SEMPER IN SPECIEM

ALWAYS FOR THE SAKE OF APPEARANCES

KEEPING UP APPEARANCES

HYACINTH BUCKET'S
Book of Etiquette
FOR THE SOCIALLY LESS FORTUNATE

BBC BOOKS

Published by BBC Books, an imprint of BBC Worldwide Publishing.
BBC Worldwide Ltd., Woodlands, 80 Wood Lane, London, W12 0TT.

First published in hardback 1993
First published in paperback 1994
Reprinted 1994 (twice), 1995

ISBN 0 563 37107 2

Designed by Hammond Hammond
Illustrations by Chris Lloyd
Jacket illustrations by Simon Roulstone
Jacket photos of Hyacinth Bucket © BBC
Background photo by John Stewart

Set in Goudy Old Style by Selwood Systems, Midsomer Norton
Printed and bound in Great Britain by Clays Ltd, St Ives plc
Cover printed by Clays Ltd, St Ives plc

PICTURE ACKNOWLEDGEMENTS

Barnaby's Picture Library 29, 48, 87, 88 (right);
Hulton Deutsch Collections 19, 40/41, 82.
All Other Photographs © BBC.

ABOUT THE AUTHORS

ROY CLARK is one of Britain's most prolific, successful and popular television authors. He has spent the most part of the last twenty-five years writing, equally successfully, both drama and situation comedy. His credits include *Open All Hours*, *Potter*, *Last of the Summer Wine* and, most recently, *Keeping-Up Appearances*. He lives in Yorkshire.

JONATHAN RICE is a writer and consultant. He has written three books on cricket, as well as others on bridge, golf and Anglo-Japanese trade. With Tim Rice and Paul Gambaccini, he is co-author of the million-selling *British Hit Singles* and related books on popular music. This is his third title for BBC Books, but the first to have such an impressive cover. He lives in Kent with his wife, three children and an uncontrollable dog.

CONTENTS

Preface

PAGE SIX

CHAPTER ONE

Etiquette in the Home

PAGE EIGHT

CHAPTER TWO

Family, Relations and Friends

PAGE THIRTY-SIX

CHAPTER THREE

Improving the Mind

PAGE SEVENTY

CHAPTER FOUR

The Perfect Hostess

PAGE NINETY-EIGHT

CHAPTER FIVE

Social Obligations

PAGE ONE HUNDRED AND TWENTY-SIX

CHAPTER SIX

A Healthy Mind in a Healthy Body

PAGE ONE HUNDRED AND FIFTY-EIGHT

Index

PAGE ONE HUNDRED AND NINETY

PREFACE

Dear Reader,

It is with some trepidation that I have decided to give in to the pleas of my public and create the definitive work on modern social behaviour. I am, after all, known for my knowledge of what is right on all occasions. My family all turn to me for advice. 'Ring Hyacinth,' they say. 'She'll know.' It gets very wearing, but I know my social obligations.

What is more, since it became known that I was intending to put pen to paper (personally embossed, pastel blue with matching envelopes) to clear up many of those silly little everyday problems of etiquette and personal behaviour, I have been inundated with letters from people both known and unknown, begging me to share my own unique wisdom with them, so that they will always know what to do and what not to do in times of social indecision. Of course, it has been a strain on the Post Office having to deal with even larger than usual postal deliveries to our house, but at least it has also meant that the postman now understands who is the most important resident in the Avenue.

Rather than try to answer every query individually, which would only further overload an already inefficient postal delivery service, I have included many of these questions in this little book of mine, and I have dealt with them as fully as my editor will permit, illustrating the pertinent points with

anecdotes from my own hectic schedule. Incidentally, I have noticed one or two things about my editor. For a start, she does not always wear a smart dress with pearls and matching handbag to our editorial meetings, but at least that means there is no danger of our outfits clashing. On occasions she has even been seen to drink coffee from a BBC beaker, but I have felt it unwise to point out all her shortcomings to her. She will recognize her errors when she reads my manuscript, which was written with a gold-nibbed fountain-pen containing a blue-black ink by appointment to Her Majesty.

I have also tried to cope with some of the more socially barren aspects of our modern existence, as embodied in my dear sister Daisy and her husband Onslow, whose attitude to life is casual to the point of recklessness. This is merely to serve as an awful warning to those who feel that they do not have an obligation to rise up from the surroundings in which they were born, especially if those surroundings have subsequently been enhanced by the addition of an abandoned car containing a large and unpedigreed dog – but I shan't dwell upon this now.

I am sure that I can say of this book that, as I often remark to Richard before one of our candlelight suppers, 'It's going to be the usual success.' It will teach you more than you ever need to know.

Hyacinth Bucket

CHAPTER ONE

ETIQUETTE IN THE HOME

I LIKE TO THINK of myself as just a typical British housewife living in a typical British detached house with net curtains, a well-behaved garden and Westminster chimes on the doorbell. It may well be the smartest house in our modestly elegant but secluded Avenue, but that is merely because our typical neighbours do not rise to the challenge as I do. A typical British housewife has a responsibility to herself and her family to maintain certain standards of behaviour, deportment and dress, and I make it my duty to achieve these standards, come what may. My family and neighbours may from time to time stray from the highest levels of social etiquette, but I and my Royal Doulton tableware will not.

People often ask how I manage to keep up my hectic schedule of engagements and maintain such a high level of correctness in all I do. I sometimes overhear my brother-in-law Onslow – he is the type of man who sings on coach trips, so you can quickly understand what sort of a man I have to deal with – saying, almost in awe, 'How does Hyacinth do it? Chuff me, how does she do it?'

In writing this book, I will try to let you in on some of my most precious secrets, so that you too will learn how to become

HYACINTH BUCKET'S
Book of Etiquette

(Above) A typical British housewife
(Left) The type of man who sings on coach
trips

the focus of your neighbourhood, and to be considered as central to your own social whirl as I am to ours. I fear there may be too many words and too few pictures for Onslow to get through to the end, but I am of the opinion that he is probably beyond redemption anyway. If I can persuade my publishers to put a nice romantic picture on the cover, then at least my sister Daisy may borrow it from the library. Her fundamental family instincts of beauty and order seem recently to have been eclipsed by Onslow's overwhelming presence and a rising tide of empty beer cans and moulting dogs. However, I know my dear husband Richard will read it: I will give it to him for his next birthday, signed by the authoress, with best wishes.

There is a saying that charity begins at home, although in my experience it begins at the church hall with a bring-and-buy sale or a short musical concert for the elderly of the parish, with dear Emmet playing the piano while I entertain with a medley of songs from 'The Sound of Music'. But more of that anon. What is certain is that good etiquette begins at home, so that is where we shall start.

A home is more than just bricks and mortar. The house wherein reside my sisters Rose and Daisy and our dear courageous Daddy, not to mention Onslow, is the exception to this rule, being rather less than just bricks and mortar, but the lesson to be learnt is that there is a great difference between a house and a home. A house is just a building in which some people live. A home is a smart, well-decorated house with a newly-emulsioned dining-room ceiling and a private pearl-white slimline push button telephone in the hall. A home has crystal glassware, and a portrait of Sir Winston Churchill on the wall;

There is a great deal of difference
between a house and a home

it has wallpaper against which tradespeople do not brush, and it has monthly magazines with articles about royalty and cooking aubergines neatly displayed on the coffee table. It has a comprehensively polished motor-car in the drive. It is a place where candlelight suppers can be held with confidence.

A home begins at the front door. As I have remarked to my dear neighbour Elizabeth time and again, I think it is so common, using back doors. The proper way for my guests, I always feel, is through the front door. Even if we then go straight to the kitchen (as I always do, unless it is someone special), I feel that the front door is the proper way into and out of a real home. There are often difficulties in maintaining such strict rules, but it is always worth it. I remember one time when Elizabeth was enjoying a leisurely cup of coffee in our recently refitted kitchen, having only spilt a few biscuit crumbs on the floor, and the telephone rang. It was my sister Violet – large house, sauna, room for a pony – reporting to me the fact that her husband Bruce was up a tree, sulking and wearing her best evening dress. As I put the telephone back in its slimline cradle, I felt it was probably time for Elizabeth to leave.

A home begins at the front door

'Finished already, dear?' I enquired, taking her beaker from her with just the right degree of firmness and solicitude.

'Apparently,' said Elizabeth. 'Well, yes. Then I must be going.'

One of the signs of true politeness is an awareness of the feelings of others, and this Elizabeth displays to a laudable degree. Sometimes I wonder whether she is too precisely aware

My dear neighbour Elizabeth

of my feelings, but I believe that most of the time, thankfully, she is not. She got up and made for the back door.

'No, no. Not through the back door, dear. Good gracious me, whatever kind of a friend would I be to send you creeping out through the back door? No, come along. We'll use the front door.'

'I don't mind the back door, Hyacinth,' said Elizabeth, whose standards as a hostess are obviously not as high as mine.

'Well I do, dear. For my friends.' I led the way to our front door, making sure that neither of us brushed against the hall wallpaper. I have a terrible feeling that there are traces of Onslow on my hall wallpaper, but at least there are none of Elizabeth. I opened the front door gracefully.

'Do have a look at the tulips on your way out dear.'

It was at this moment that a cloud appeared in what otherwise were the clear blue skies of a fine May day. Daisy and Onslow entered our drive, pushing an empty wheelchair. They were not dressed to receive company. Daisy was still wearing her slippers and Onslow's tattoos were exposed to the elements and the gaze of all in the Avenue. It would have been entirely inappropriate to use that moment to make formal introductions between my sister and her husband, and my dear neighbour Elizabeth. The mark of a fine hostess, however, is to be able to think quickly.

'Come to think of it, the tulips in the back garden are far superior,' I said, before Elizabeth had spotted the new arrivals. We turned around and Elizabeth left through the back door. There are times when one's principles have to be compromised if the veneer of gracious living is to remain unscratched.

Perhaps the biggest problem with having a perfectly decorated house is that of tradespersons. Milkmen, postmen, television

Ah yes, I thought I heard the milkman

Dear Milkman,

I do like these bright spring mornings, don't you? It must give you particular pleasure to be able to wander freely in your remarkable electric vehicle, delivering milk and other dairy products to the good citizens of the neighbourhood.

I do not want you to think me even in the slightest bit critical of the fine job you have to do, but I would certainly be most grateful if, on those mornings when you clatter around before first light, you could dispense with whistling selections from the Hit Parade. If you must give vent to your musical feelings, take the advice of someone with music in her veins, someone who would have trod the professional boards if only she had followed the pleadings of her contemporaries in her younger days: just hum a few bars of a Strauss Waltz, or an aria from 'The White Horse Inn'. None of these tuneless 'pop' tunes in our Avenue, please.

Incidentally, the reason I did not go on to the stage, despite public demand, was because I followed my heart into marriage and motherhood. But do not presume that I am any less a true music professional merely because I do not take encores every night at Drury Lane.

And an extra strawberry yoghurt, please.

Hyacinth Bucket

repairmen, electricity meter readers all come to the front door and expect at the very least to involve themselves in conversation with the lady of the house. Often they expect to gain admittance to the premises in the course of their duties.

It is most important that these tradespersons understand the social hierarchy, and their place in it. The likes of Richard and I are put in well-appointed residences in tree-lined avenues in order to be served, and tradespeople are put in uniform to serve us. It is our obligation to ensure that they give the best service they can. The milkman, for example, must understand that the milk he delivers to the Bucket household should be of a quite different quality to that (or *from* that? I am never quite sure) delivered to Mr Hislop at number 43, for example. The other day I happened to hear a gentle clink of bottles as I was arranging some dahlias in our bone china vase by the front door just before breakfast. My skills in flower arrangement are often remarked upon, and I find my artistic talent flares up at any time of the day, craving to be immediately assuaged: it is so obvious where our dear son Sheridan gets his temperament from.

I unlocked the front door and caught sight of the milkman retreating halfway down our drive.

'Ah yes! I thought I heard the milkman.'

'How?' he asked, rather aggressively I thought. 'I'd like to know how you heard the milkman. You must have radar.'

'No, thank you,' I replied, fixing him with a superior but friendly stare. 'My usual two pints and the occasional yoghurt is all I require. You are quite sure my milk went into a clean bottle?'

The milkman came back towards me, wiped his hands on

his overalls and presented them to me for inspection. I turned them over to look at both front and back.

'Very good. I do like a milkman with clean fingernails. You bring me an extra yoghurt tomorrow. You see how cleanliness pays.'

'An extra yoghurt! Wow! What flavour?' I felt that perhaps the milkman was not taking the good news of this extra piece of business as seriously as he should have done.

'Surprise me.'

'I'd love to.'

'By the way,' I added, as the milkman tried once again to slip away, 'I'm still waiting for an answer to my query.'

'What query was that, Mrs Bucket?'

'It's Bouquet.' How many times do I have to repeat what should be an obvious pronunciation to all who see the name written down.

'I never knew that. To me people are usually just a name on a note.'

That is just too much. Do tradespersons not understand that we, the customers, are their livelihood?

'I will not have milkmen reducing me to a piece of paper.' The milkman fidgeted awkwardly with the two empty milk bottles and a plastic packet of potatoes which for some reason he was carrying. 'I wanted your superiors to find out which cow my milk came from. I will not have my bottles coming from just any old animal. We passed a very photogenic herd recently, grazing on the Earl of Crawford's estate. Would you please ensure that in future my two pints daily come from them.'

'All the milk's been tested, Mrs Buc – er, Bouquet.'

A very photogenic herd of cows,
grazing on the Earl of Crawford's estate

'I should hope so. Just remember two pints of it are destined for some very high quality china.'

The lesson to be learned here is that the socially aware hostess is always firm but completely fair with people in trade. It is not necessarily their fault that they have not qualified in one of the professions, or have been as successful as my Richard in Local Authority circles. We must always expect the very best from those who exist to provide us with services, and never let

them relax in their duties. This is something which is always appreciated in the long run.

I think I have the electricity-meter man well-trained, but it did take some time. He came a few weeks ago while I was on the telephone, so Elizabeth, who had just finished breaking one of Grandmama's teacups, answered the door for me.

'It's the electric man. To read your meter,' she called.

'Is it the one with the funny moustache?' I am never quite certain about facial hair. Richard, of course, has a moustache, but it is not an oppressive growth. It adds distinction to his upper lip without blanketing it with rampant follicles. The electric man has a less well-manicured moustache.

Richard's moustache is not an oppressive growth

'He says yes.'

'Make him wait there until I've looked at his feet.'

By the time I had finished my telephone conversation, the electric man was standing by the front door mat with his shoes in his hand.

'Oh, the shoes! You remembered our procedure last time. Leave them outside and do come in. Close the door. The heat's on.'

This man is a great improvement on his predecessor. The

last one used to brush against my walls. Of course I rang his superiors. I told them, I said I will not have an electric man brushing against my walls. In fact, I will not have any type of tradesman brushing against my walls. I remember the time when we were expecting the delivery of a new three-piece suite which is the exact replica of one at Sandringham House. Even though the delivery vans all had the royal warrant on both sides, so that they could be clearly seen by the Barker-Finches at number 23, I was not prepared for their employees to brush against my walls in the course of their work. How does one overcome this particular problem? One uses one's husband.

I am particularly lucky in this respect. Dear Richard is always keen to help me solve even the thorniest of social problems. 'Come on, Richard. I want you to anticipate where delivery men of average height are liable to brush against my walls. Even if they do possess the royal warrant, I expect you to prevent it, Richard.'

'How am I supposed to stop them brushing against your walls?'

Really, sometimes Richard is so helpless.

'By inserting yourself between the delivery man and the wallpaper.'

However, it is not just wallpaper one needs to be concerned about whenever the delivering classes are involved. It is also important, for example, to make sure that electric men do not touch meter cupboard handles. One never knows in whose houses they may previously have touched meter cupboard handles, without subsequently washing thoroughly with soap and water.

'Ah-ah-ah-aah, fingers!' is the standard way of playfully reminding such people not to touch.

When the electric man, or the gas man come to that, reads the meter, it is important to ensure a correct reading. I find that checking their reading over their shoulder tends to keep them on the straight and narrow.

I also like to keep them on their toes as far as the quality of their product is concerned. 'Is your electricity as clean as it was, do you think? My hobs are sometimes very difficult to clean.'

'Cleanest fuel there is.'

'But it goes to some very funny families. Would you have mine checked to make quite sure that I get it first? I won't have it if it's already been to some of those other places.'

'Leave it with me, lady.'

A member of the delivering classes

Of course, the lot of a trades-person is not always a happy one. They are not always lucky enough to be given an area which includes the upper end of Avenue society. Those who have to deal with Daisy and Onslow and poor Daddy have a much harder time of it. It's the dustbin men I feel especially sorry for. I mean, how can they distinguish between what they are supposed to take and what's supposed to stay?

At this point, let me bring in the very first of the hundreds of letters from my eager public. Ever since word leaked out through publishing circles that I was to let the world in on some of my secrets of social living, my poor postman has been forced into stopping more than once a day at our house. It has long been common knowledge that we receive more mail than those next door, but sometimes in the past, our mail has been mislaid in the depths of the sorting office, so that, for example, the card my sister Violet sent me from Tenerife never arrived. Over these past few months, however, they have needed to create a special pigeonhole in the post office for the Bucket residence.

What is the main difference in style and attitude between those members of the Avenue set and mere ordinary folk? asks a correspondent, on heavily scented vellum notepaper, the smell of which is perhaps just a little too forthright to stay within the bounds of good taste.

Let me answer that by giving an example from one of our many hectic social rounds. When we were chosen by Mrs Fortescue – the old lady who's virtually aristocracy – above all her acquaintances blessed with their own transport, to give her a lift into town, it was hard to persuade Richard to approach her house in the correct frame of mind. We rehearsed the ringing of the bell at our own front door before we left. Richard pressed the bell, and the Westminster chimes pealed out diffidently.

'Oh no, not like that, Richard. That was almost a trades-man's ring. Keep the index finger straight. For my sake, Richard, please practise your ring. It should be firm but friendly.' There in a nutshell, dear reader, is the difference in style and attitude between the well-bred members of society and the *hoi polloi*. In life everything should be firm but friendly, not oafish or

Richard has the friendliness,
but lacks the firmness

obsequious as seems to be the present-day trend.

Richard is just too tentative. He has the friendliness, but lacks the firmness. When introducing himself, he should have made Mrs Fortescue realize he was a power in Local Authority circles. His ridiculous response was to say, 'Couldn't I just say, "Good morning, Mrs Fortescue", and I'll wear a large label saying "Powerful In Local Authority Circles"?' He often tries to spoil things with middle-class humour.

*W*hat *is the right way to use the telephone?* asks another confused correspondent. I note that she sent her query in by mail, rather than risking making further *faux pas* (that's French, you know, the exact translation of which need not concern us here) by using the very instrument she is so uncertain of.

There are of course two right ways to use the telephone, and neither of them resemble the advice given to me by some uncouth man who had rung our pearl-white slimline number in the mistaken hope of ordering a Chinese meal. I have no idea what good the telephone would have been up my jumper, anyway, even if I had been wearing one at the time, which I was not.

1. The first way to use the telephone is when answering an incoming call. A warm greeting such as 'The Bouquet residence. The lady of the house speaking,' is the correct way to answer the telephone's urgent ring. It is, of course, of the utmost importance that one is dressed to receive telephone calls. I will never forget the ignominy of Richard answering the telephone in our bedroom without his trousers on and his garters showing, and the caller was a lady too. He really must be more careful. 'You shouldn't be answering the phone to ladies in that condition,' I told him. My youngest sister Rose is a liability on the telephone as well. Whenever I talk to her I have to remind her to wear something sensible. It always makes me very nervous to think I might be talking to a mini-skirt.

· The Art of the Telephone ·

Rose is a very talented telephone conversationalist. She is able to keep her mind on several things at once, even at moments of great personal tragedy. There was one occasion when Rose was opening her heart to me down the telephone line while at the same time fixing an eyelash. Onslow was watching the horseracing on television, buried under a large volume of unpedigreed dog.

Rose is a very talented telephone conversationalist

'I can't live without Mr Hepplewhite,' she cried, even though the eyelash was threatening to come unstuck.

'Will you keep it down, Rose,' shouted Onslow in the background.

'I can't live without Mr Hepplewhite,' she whispered. 'Not since the tragedy. It's what happens to all men in the end. He's gone back to his wife. I have to die. I threatened him I would.'

At this point I clearly heard Onslow's voice again.

'What do you fancy in the three o'clock?'

'Rainbow Lady,' said Rose, before getting to the main point of her call. 'I want to be buried in Mother's wedding dress.' In her world, the three o'clock race takes precedence over attempted suicide.

The second way to use the telephone correctly is when making an outgoing call. It is absolutely vital to make sure you get through to the people who matter. It is no good settling for second best. 'Firm but friendly' is the motto here too. I remember on one occasion I had cause to telephone the Prime Minister. It was not an easy task.

'Hello? Is that the Prime Minister's office? Well, would you put me through to the Prime Minister's office, please?' There

Hello? Is that the Prime Minister's office?

was a pause during which I gave them the benefit of several bars of 'I Am Sixteen Going On Seventeen'. 'Ah, finally. It's worse than trying to get through to British Rail Enquiries. My business is confidential, so I wish to be put through to someone important. That is to say, not a minor functionary. I will not be fobbed off with a minor functionary.'

'What is your name, please, madam?' asked the minor functionary.

'My name is Bouquet. B-U-C-K-E-T. The matter is confidential.'

'Hold on a moment, madam.' I resumed at the third chorus of 'I Am Sixteen Going On Seventeen' while waiting to be connected with a less minor functionary. By the time a voice finally came onto the line, I had completed all but two bars of the third verse, and had eliminated two off-colour daffodils from the vase on the table in the hall.

'Ah, hello. You are the third private secretary? Who does one have to be to get through to numbers one and two? However, yes, you can help me. I'd like a little advance information, about the Honours List. My husband is retiring after a lifetime of public service and I am assuming of course that there will be something for him in the Honours List. Now I know you are not supposed to blurt these things out, but a little hint in the strictest confidence would be greatly appreciated. I don't want to have to learn about it from the newspapers. As a meticulous hostess, I'd like to be prepared. It's going to mean redecorating for a start.'

3 Then there is the third way of using the telephone, but this is never the right way. The third
way is when duty forces me to telephone my
dear sisters Daisy and Rose to find out about the
delicate state of health of my dear Daddy, only
to find that the telephone is picked up by Onslow. This can have
an unsettling effect on even the best modulated telephone lines.

'Oh it's you, Onslow. How are you?' This question is always
a tactical error. 'You needn't go into detail. It was merely an
enquiry about your general health. I'm sorry you have a mosquito bite but its location is really none of my business despite
our being related by marriage.' He has the most graphic powers
of description for a man with so little formal education. 'Yes,
Onslow, I'm sure most people do wonder how you manage to
get bitten there, but that's not the kind of speculation I care to
pursue. Thank you, Onslow. That's quite enough of the coarse
remarks. I wish to converse with my sister.'

'Good morning, Daisy dear. What was Onslow wearing?'
She told me the bad news. 'I hate talking to Onslow when he's
only wearing a vest. No wonder he gets mosquito bites in odd
places.'

Another enquiry: *How does one maintain standards
in the neighbourhood?* Well, there's a sweeping question if ever I heard one. But it concerns us all. I clearly remember
a conversation with Richard – it was the morning when I first

Elizabeth has a man in the house

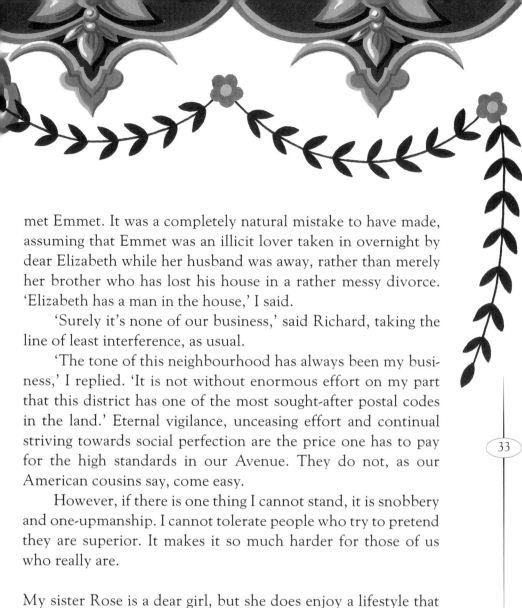

met Emmet. It was a completely natural mistake to have made, assuming that Emmet was an illicit lover taken in overnight by dear Elizabeth while her husband was away, rather than merely her brother who has lost his house in a rather messy divorce. 'Elizabeth has a man in the house,' I said.

'Surely it's none of our business,' said Richard, taking the line of least interference, as usual.

'The tone of this neighbourhood has always been my business,' I replied. 'It is not without enormous effort on my part that this district has one of the most sought-after postal codes in the land.' Eternal vigilance, unceasing effort and continual striving towards social perfection are the price one has to pay for the high standards in our Avenue. They do not, as our American cousins say, come easy.

However, if there is one thing I cannot stand, it is snobbery and one-upmanship. I cannot tolerate people who try to pretend they are superior. It makes it so much harder for those of us who really are.

My sister Rose is a dear girl, but she does enjoy a lifestyle that precludes clean living. Sharing a house with Onslow and Daisy cannot be good training for a woman with a naturally casual mind, either, but even she sees the error of their ways from time to time. That's not to say that I do not love my sisters. Of course I do. It's just that I always find myself hoping that they do not offer us a cup of tea whenever we visit them. Richard agrees with me.

'I like your Daisy. She's a very generous, warm soul.'
'I like my Daisy. I'm just not very fond of her cracked mugs.'

'I like Rose, come to think of it.'

'Oh, we all know you like Rose, Richard. All the male sex like Rose. That's her trouble.'

'She's just another gentle soul really. She's just a bit mixed up.'

All the male sex like Rose. That's her trouble

She is not, however, sufficiently mixed up not to notice that Daisy is not particularly well-suited to housework. She relayed to me a conversation that took place over a breakfast of cigarettes and beer: 'I hate tidying up,' said Daisy. 'I'm under the doctor for being dizzy. I'm sure it's the tidying up.'

'If you only got dizzy when you tidied up,' retorted Rose with more than a grain of truth, 'you should have the clearest head in the area.'

Occasionally, the discussions in their house become quite philosophical, almost existential in their blithe disregard for the realities of a responsible lifestyle.

'Do we tidy up?' began Daisy.

'Let's ask Onslow. He's the master of the house.'

It goes without saying that any house which has Onslow as its master has got more problems than mere terminal untidiness,

*The possible meaninglessness of
the entire universe*

but he is never without an answer for even the most tricky debate.

'Given the transience of life, biology's awesome potential for instability, and the possible meaninglessness of the entire universe, do you think it's worth the bother?'

Daisy was impressed. 'Do you think the universe is meaningless?'

Without raising his beer can from his stomach or his head from the racing page of the newspaper, Onslow gave his verdict. 'I must say I was inclined towards that theory when I saw you wearing that see-through nightie over a vest.'

'But what about love?'

'Not right now, Daze, I'm busy.'

An incurable romantic should never marry an Onslow.

HYACINTH BUCKET'S

Book of Etiquette

CHAPTER TWO

FAMILY, RELATIONS AND FRIENDS

THE WHOLE OF our universe revolves around the joys and tribulations of family life, of that there can be little doubt. Unfortunately, in my family, there are usually more tribulations than joys, always excepting my darling Sheridan, who is everything a mother could wish her son to be. The rest of our extended family, which in the case of Onslow is usually extended along their extraordinarily tatty settee, tends to let me down more often than I would wish. As I remarked to Richard on one occasion during a family outing when we were walking several yards behind Onslow who was pushing Daddy in his wheelchair, 'I know they are my family and you know I love them dearly. But just in case any friends are passing, I think perhaps I'd like to keep that our little secret.' I am not one for ostentatious displays of good works.

That time which I may already have mentioned when we were due to take delivery of a new three-piece suite which is the exact replica of one at Sandringham House, I also offered, out of the generosity of an elder sister's heart, to let Daisy have our old three-piece suite (of less royal pedigree) which was now becoming surplus to requirements. It is a mark of fine breeding to be ready to dispose of one's old furniture amongst the socially

A Christmas portrait. Unfortunately,
Onslow could not be there

less fortunate, provided of course that they agree to come and collect the goods themselves. Sadly, on this occasion, they chose the exact moment when I was expecting delivery of the new suite, and when the Barker-Finches at number 23 must have been twitching at their net curtains in pure unbridled jealousy, to arrive in the tattiest pick-up I have ever seen. It was borrowed, it appears, from Onslow's mother's sister's son Rafe, whom he insists on calling 'my cousin Ralphie'. This is a situation which

I can always rely on my dear husband Richard
to remind me of my good intentions

can upset the most dignified of hostesses, and I will confess that there was a brief moment when my composure was ruffled.

'Get rid of them!' I suggested to Richard. I could tell from the psychic pain between my shoulder blades how sharp were the eyes behind number 23's curtains. And yet they have no right to be jealous. They are just not quite our class. She was a Barker and he was a Finch. Suddenly they are hyphenated. I cannot bear that sort of snobbery.

'But Onslow and Daisy have come for the suite. You offered

them our old suite.' Even at times of crisis, I can always rely on my dear Richard to remind me of my good intentions.

'Get rid of them! Ye Gods! With Mrs Barker-Finch watching, this is all I need. Onslow in some borrowed deathtrap of a vehicle. Get rid of them!'

'But what about the old suite?' asked Richard.

'Tell them to come back later. After dark. Providing there isn't a moon.' The practical socialite thinks of everything.

'Well I can't just ask them to go away.'

'Richard, you know I love my family, but that's no reason why I should have to acknowledge them in broad daylight.' I believe in that one brief sentence, uttered under considerable strain and probably in full view of the Barker-Finches at number 23, there lies the secret to the right way of dealing with one's family. I have a book of etiquette on my shelves (to tell the truth I have several books of etiquette on my shelves, but none of them quite reach the nub of the problem) which has a chapter on 'Family Relations' which is sub-titled 'Etiquette Under Stress'. How very true.

I come from a family of four sisters. I am, of course, the eldest and as such take responsibility for the care of our one surviving parent, dear Daddy. I have decided that the best way to care for him in his sad old age after the loss of his dear spouse, Mummy, is to allow him to live in the house where he has always lived, and for him to share it with two of his daughters, my sisters Daisy and Rose. The fact that this means he also shares it with Daisy's husband Onslow and several hundred empty cans of beer is something that I cannot help. We must all learn to take the rough with the smooth. Daddy's house is unfortunately not

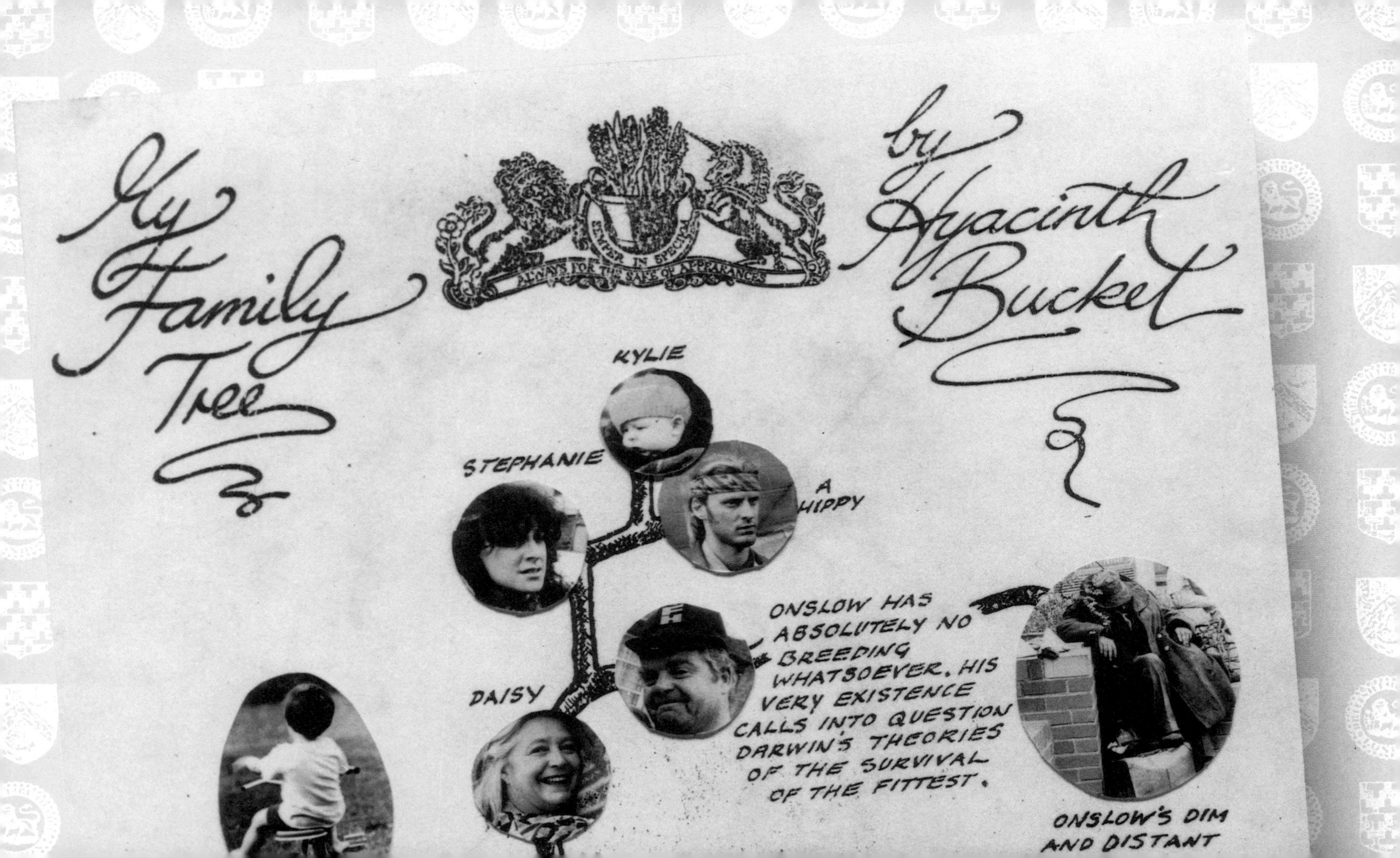

My Family Tree
by Hyacinth Bucket
SEMPER IN SPECIVM
ALWAYS FOR THE SAKE OF APPEARANCES
KYLIE
STEPHANIE
A HIPPY
DAISY
ONSLOW HAS ABSOLUTELY NO BREEDING WHATSOEVER. HIS VERY EXISTENCE CALLS INTO QUESTION DARWIN'S THEORIES OF THE SURVIVAL OF THE FITTEST.
ONSLOW'S DIM AND DISTANT

RICHARD BUCKET

SHERIDAN

HYACINTH

ROSE

BRUCE
(TURF ACCOUNTANT,
LARGE HOUSE WITH
SAUNA AND ROOM FOR
A PONY. THE LESS
SAID ABOUT BRUCE'S
PERSONAL HABITS
THE BETTER.)

POOR
MUMMY

GRANDMAMA
(HEIRLOOMS WITH
PERIWINKLES
REGULARLY
BROKEN BY
ELIZABETH
NEXT DOOR)

DADDY

GRANDPAPA

POOR BUT
HONEST ENGLISH
YEOMAN STOCK

SEVERAL
GENERATIONS OF
ARTISTIC AND MUSICAL
TALENT

ANCESTORS
WERE
EUGENICS,
I THINK,
WHICH
EXPLAINS
THE WAY
BUCKET IS
PRONOUNCED.
FOREIGN BLOOD NOW
ENTIRELY DILUTED.
WE ARE ENGLISH.

near enough to the Avenue for us to visit as often as we would wish, but I know that he is happy in the environment in which he grew up.

Daddy's later years have not been easy. He had a great mind in his day and was much respected in musical circles. But since his retirement he has allowed his sense of duty, which I have clearly inherited from him, to take him into difficult situations, such as the time when some unscrupulous female from the Senior Citizen's Club attempted to manoeuvre Daddy to the steps of the altar, or in this particular case, to the steps of the Registry Office. Fortunately for all concerned, Daddy remained asleep throughout the crisis, which showed how uninterested he was in the demands of the flesh, and how well his sedatives were working.

Onslow seems to believe that Daddy desires a more active life, but he clearly misconstrues his actions. He has even managed to get my sisters to believe the worst about their father, but then perhaps they do not care for him in the way I do.

'He's a dirty old man,' said Onslow once, when we were discussing Daddy's temporary hospitalization after having been fished out of the canal. Sometimes I wonder if it is right to leave Daddy under the same roof as Onslow, but then again, where else could he go? Nobody else wants Onslow.

'He's in love with the milkwoman,' said Rose.

'Don't be so ridiculous,' I snorted. As if my daddy could fall for someone with such a poor foothold on the social ladder as a milkwoman.

'He pedalled after her for a mile down by the canal, stark naked on his bike.'

'You know how fond he is of dairy products,' I replied. 'I expect he wanted to order some more cream.'

When I got to the hospital, it was clear that my initial diagnosis was correct. I asked the doctor in what condition my father was when he was admitted, and a rather oafish man in the next bed, wearing a cloth cap and looking too fit to be anything

How well Daddy's sedatives are working

other than a malingerer, shouted, 'Drunk as a skunk.'

What a pity Daddy let his private medical insurance lapse. He should not be forced to share his Intensive Care facilities with anybody wearing a cloth cap.

'I expect he was flushed from excessive cycling,' I suggested. 'Can you describe what he was wearing, doctor?'

'Very quickly,' said the doctor. 'He was wearing very little really. To be honest, nothing at all.'

'He'd been in the canal,' interrupted the malingerer again. 'He was that plastered he wobbled off into the canal.'

'Well, that explains it. My father was cycling along the canal, when he saw someone in distress. So he removed his outer garments and dived in to save them.' I gazed fondly at my father, lying sedated in his bed. 'How brave, Daddy.'

For many years, Daddy and Mummy were the perfect couple. Mummy had inherited from her Mummy, my Grandmama, not only her cups with hand-painted periwinkles, but also a love of music and art, which has in turn been passed on to me and through me to my dear Sheridan. I miss Mummy terribly, as Daddy does too, of course.

Let me turn once again to my pile of correspondence. I fear I am not getting through it as quickly as I had expected. Each letter leads me along paths I had not anticipated.

My dear Hyacinth, the letter begins, *what is the derivation of your most interesting name?*

Perhaps I should begin my reply by mentioning that until we have been formally introduced, I am not your 'dear Hyacinth'. In fact, I doubt if I would be even after we have been formally introduced, madam, but all the same, your question is an interesting one.

HYACINTH BUCKET'S
Book of Etiquette

Three sisters, in full bloom

Mummy loved flowers and for that reason she chose to name her daughters after the blooms that appeared in our splendid garden. I, the first-born, was named Hyacinth, which shows a prescience that only now is something to be appreciated. A hyacinth, as all my green-fingered readers will be aware, is a flower of exquisite perfume which blooms best indoors. I am a home person, the mistress of a fine house constantly ablaze with candlelight suppers and tea parties with canapés. I bloom in the social environment. I am a true hyacinth.

My sister Daisy was the next to come along. Like most Daisies, she is a bit of a wild flower. I like to think of her as Olearia, the daisy bush, which is a hardy specimen that flourishes in windswept environments. Daisy is certainly a hardy specimen: you would have to be to cope with Onslow, and I cannot imagine that her house is swept by anything but wind. She has that rather spontaneously assembled look that goes with her name.

The two youngest are Violet and Rose. The violet, or pansy is 'free-flowering for bold effects', according to my book, *Precise Gardening for the Orderly Woman*. In Violet's case it is her husband Bruce, or pansy, that is free-flowering for effects that are far too bold, even in a man who has provided her with a Mercedes and a sauna. There may be room for a pony in Violet's garden, but I am not sure there is room for a man who likes to dress in his wife's best ball gown.

Rose, my youngest sister, was carefully named. Although *Precise Gardening for the Orderly Woman* tells me that roses 'go back into unrecorded time, before man himself', I am sure my sister Rose would not have been happy in a time before there were men. But the rose is the best-loved flower, and Rose has

*Stephanie with baby Kylie and,
perhaps, Kylie's father*

been loved by the best. And the worst. But as sisters, we do still agree on the basic principles of life, however carefully Rose appears to disguise them. I well remember her saying to me, on more than one occasion, 'I've finished with men. They are nothing but heartache and trouble.'

'I know what you mean,' I replied tenderly. 'I can never get Richard to fold his pyjamas.'

Of course, the person over whom the most thought was given when it came to a name was my darling Sheridan. Daisy's daughter is called Stephanie, a name that anybody could have thought of, which is proved by the fact that Onslow did. And Stephanie went so far as to name her own daughter Kylie. What kind of name is that for a Christian person? It sounds like a foreign vegetable.

But I digress. Our Sheridan was bound to be artistic, given his genealogy, especially on his mother's side. So despite Richard's views that something more ordinary like John or David would be more acceptable, we agreed to name our son after that fine writer and politician Richard Brinsley Sheridan, who lived some years ago, I believe. It was he who put into words in his

My Sheridan is a keen cyclist

play, *The Critic*, the spirit that should be the driving force for all lovers of the social order, 'I must – I will – I can – I ought – I do.' All that I do, I do because I must. I can do it because I ought to do it. So I will. And so does Sheridan.

*W*hat *is the correct way to cope with a gifted son?* This of course is not a point of etiquette that will apply to all my readers, but coping with a gifted son is something that I have great experience of, having prepared for it all my life. There are some things in life that one knows are inevitable, like my mothering a son who would be exceptionally gifted, and so it was something I was ready for. As I have remarked many times before, and will probably do so again, I never like leaving things to chance. It is the mark of a thoughtful mother. But it would unnerve some mothers how exceptional Sheridan is. As a baby his musical appreciation was extra-ordinary. Even as a tiny child, when I sang it could reduce him to tears. And he has such natural good taste. My Mummy, he often boasted, designs the perfect salad. I used to protest – covered with embarrassment in the way that lesser salad tossers would be covered with spring onions and bits of lettuce – but that is how he was: so perceptive even at that age.

He's always had good taste, even as quite a small child, so it was important that his mummy could match his natural appreciation of the order of things. When other boys would come home from school looking as though they had barely

My Mummy designs the perfect salad

survived an explosion, my Sheridan would still have his tie on straight, and the cleanest pair of knees in the civilized world. And he's very persistent and self-disciplined. I remember his scoutmaster saying he had never seen anyone apply more grit and determination to the acquisition of his cook's badge than Sheridan.

He is obviously destined for high places. I just thank my lucky stars he is blessed with a mother who will be able to cope with the demands of his future position. We retain a close psychic link, so that I always know when it is his ring on the private slimline white telephone. It must be a great comfort to him to know however high he rises I shall be there beside him, ready to take the social strain. I could handle all his entertaining. It is as if I have been in training all my life. When the call comes, I shall be there.

We now move on to the thorny subject of marriage. *Should a marriage*, asks an uncertain spinster among my followers, *be a lifelong love affair or a social alliance?*

Well, of course, a lifelong love affair can be rather awkward when it comes to good behaviour in public. One does not like to see people of the opposite gender intertwining all over the place, whether or not they are married. It just does not make for good conversation. However, I have been fortunate. In my marriage to Richard, I have enjoyed not only the lasting comfort of a good man by my side (or occasionally two paces behind

*A perfect partnership of social
connections and good looks*

me), but also the social status that comes with being married to a manager within the Local Authority. And without any more intertwining than is strictly necessary.

When I first met Richard, he was a young man with a neatly trimmed moustache and a fine button-up grey woollen cardigan. I was a shy young thing with little experience of life, despite the responsibility of raising three younger sisters after Mummy was called to be an angel. His enthusiasm for life and his great plans for the future just swept me off my feet, I suppose. It was inevitable that such a man would be looking for a fine woman of impeccable background to be his helpmeet throughout life's troublesome journey, and so it must have been more than mere fate that led our paths to cross. It was, of course, a grand passion. Within five years of that first meeting, we were married, and on our honeymoon it was wonderful

His enthusiasm for life just swept me off my feet, I suppose

to be able to dispense with the services of a chaperone at last. We lived those seven heady days in Weston-super-Mare to the full, and ever since then our marriage has been a perfect partnership of organizational skills, social connections and good looks, coupled with Richard's willingness to learn.

My dear next door neighbour Emmet, who has not had

many good experiences of marriage himself but I am sure it is not entirely his fault, once asked his sister after one of my most successful cocktails and canapés parties, 'Where does Richard get his reserves of courage?'

Elizabeth replied, 'Well, Richard has a very patient and kindly nature, also I think he lives in a quiet little world of his own.'

'He deserves the Nobel Prize for Peace,' said Emmet. He is a most generous and musically competent neighbour, but even I think that was going too far. I have often wondered why my Richard has not yet been honoured with an OBE or some such for his services to the community through his senior managerial position within the Finance and General Services department of the Local Authority, but not even I had thought of the Nobel Prize.

'They are a very close couple,' added Elizabeth.

I did not quite catch Emmet's response as I had to say goodbye to Major Wilton-Smythe but it could not have been what it sounded like: 'Of course they are close, she has him on a lead.'

Daisy and Onslow have a marriage that can hardly be described as a social alliance, but at least they have a marriage (which is more than I can say for their daughter Stephanie). When Daddy was under threat of a second marriage because of the presence of a strange woman in his bedroom, Daisy went to investigate.

'What's going on?' I asked, when she returned from the inner depths of her appalling home.

'Nothing. She's just sitting there without moving,' said Daisy. 'I thought for a minute it was Onslow.'

*No more intertwining than
is strictly necessary*

*An atmosphere that crackles
with sexual tension*

'It's remarks like that,' said her husband, 'which help to cool the first furious fires of a marriage.'

Yet Onslow himself is not always the romantic. Daisy once suggested to Onslow that he grow a moustache. His response was typical of him: 'You want a moustache; why don't you grow a moustache?'

Daisy was not to be put off. 'I'd just like some little sign that you were trying to exert an attraction over me, Onslow. A woman likes to be wooed. She should live in an atmosphere that crackles with sexual tension.'

In thirty years of marriage the atmosphere has never once crackled with sexual tension

I am afraid that here, for once, I have to take Onslow's side. I am pleased to report that in thirty years of marriage with Richard, the atmosphere has never once crackled, or even fizzled, with sexual tension.

*W*hen visiting one's family members, what is the correct procedure? Should one always be invited, or is it permissible just to turn up on the doorstep?

I am very pleased to have the opportunity to answer this particular question, because too often my own family arrive unannounced at our home, and even though they are close blood relations, my hectic social schedule is such that it is not always entirely convenient to see them, especially within the hours of daylight. When I visit my sister Daisy, I always like to give plenty of advance notice. This gives them an opportunity to tidy up the house a little, but I regret to say they all too rarely take that opportunity.

Perhaps the important thing to remember about visiting sisters who have made no attempt to work their way up the sweeping marble staircases of society is never to accept the offer of a lift to their house from a next door neighbour.

There was once a time of particular crisis when a visit had to be made to poor Daddy, but Richard was unable, because of the awesome responsibilities of his profession, to take me to my father's side. I therefore had to call on the good nature of Elizabeth, who was only too keen to offer me a lift in her little car. I expect she was flattered to be offered the chance to be seen in a private vehicle with somebody of my status.

'I don't think I've ever been to your sister Daisy's house, Hyacinth, have I?' asked Elizabeth, allowing her concentration to waver from the road ahead.

'No . . . no. You've never seen my sister Daisy's house, have you Elizabeth?' I was beginning to consider that in order to spare Daisy's blushes, it would be best if Elizabeth continued not having seen my sister's house.

'Is it a nice house?' asked Elizabeth. My mind was considering the best way to avoid the shame Daisy would be bound to feel if Elizabeth saw the tragic way that Onslow had condemned her to a life without net curtains or flock wallpaper. I remember Onslow once complaining that watching television was not the same outside your own cosy environment.

*Sisters who have made no attempt to work their way up
the sweeping marble staircases of society*

'We're not cosy,' Daisy had replied. 'We're nearly derelict.'

'I like derelict.' Her husband glowed with proprietorial pride. 'I'm into derelict.'

I did not, however, think that Elizabeth would be into derelict. 'Well, I'd really rather we were going to my sister

I'm into derelict

Violet's,' I said. 'You remember Violet. The one who married
the turf accountant who built her that big house with the sauna,
and room for a pony. You've heard me speak of Violet.'

'Frequently,' said Elizabeth. I am glad that she understands
that some members of my family besides myself know how to
live graciously.

'Violet also has a burglar alarm and an ornamental pool.
You'd like Violet's.'

'Maybe I will like Daisy's.'

'Possibly.' But I was now even more sure that poor Daisy, not to mention dear Daddy, would be mortified to have to introduce someone as clumsy but well-meaning as Elizabeth into their environment of empty beer cans and girdles under the sofa cushions. Action was required by a caring eldest sister.

'What kind of house is Daisy's?'

We were driving down a pleasant tree-lined avenue, blessed on either side by large detached properties. Inspiration suddenly struck.

'Actually, it's quite like one of these. In fact it is very like one of these, come to think of it, it is one of these. Slow down. Yes, this is it.'

I got out of the car, and told Elizabeth not to move. 'I won't invite you in, in case Daddy's contracted something unsightly.'

Although I had thus solved the problem of Daisy's loss of face with Elizabeth, who will now always believe that I have two sisters who live in substantial abodes, I was then presented with the problem of how to get from the large property with a rather straggly honeysuckle climbing up a slightly off-centre trellis on the front wall, to Daisy's house perhaps a quarter of a mile away. But geography has always been one of my strong points. From the age of seven I could name the capital of France and recite six uses of flax in the developing world, so it was a simple matter of following my well-defined sense of direction across the lawn of this strange house (I noticed some moss and three dead leaves out of place: Richard would never be allowed to introduce such informality into our garden), and up onto their garden shed and over the back wall. It was rather difficult to make my way over the wall without displacing my hat a little, but of course I did

Book of Etiquette

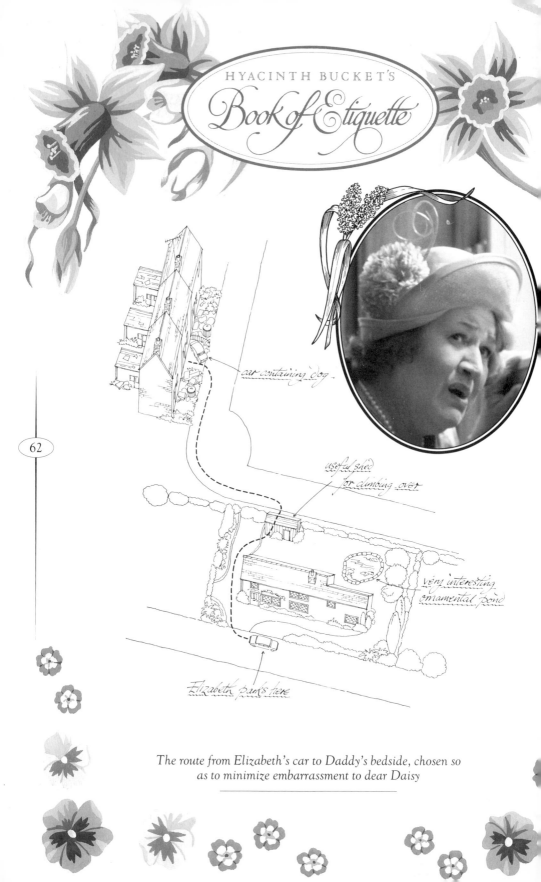

car containing dog

useful shed
for climbing over

very interesting
ornamental pond

Elizabeth parks here

*The route from Elizabeth's car to Daddy's bedside, chosen so
as to minimize embarrassment to dear Daisy*

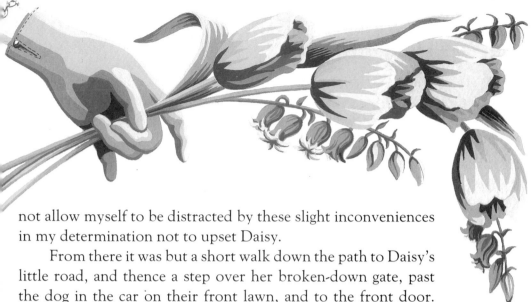

not allow myself to be distracted by these slight inconveniences in my determination not to upset Daisy.

From there it was but a short walk down the path to Daisy's little road, and thence a step over her broken-down gate, past the dog in the car on their front lawn, and to the front door. When visiting relatives, it is important not only to get there, but also to ensure that most people have little idea where you are going or how you got there. It saves so much trouble in the long run.

I am always concerned about buying the right presents for my family. How do you decide on the correct birthday gifts for your many relatives?

Ah yes, the old problem of gift-giving. Well, of course, now that this book is in the shops, you will always have the answer to that particular problem, at least amongst those in your family who can read. But if you have a relative anything like Onslow, then a suitable birthday present is far more of a challenge.

Celebrating Onslow's birthday is a perennial tribulation. Without hurting any feelings, I always feel it would be better to take a back seat at this particular festivity, and let Daisy and Onslow and their social circle enjoy the day in their own peculiar way. I was saying as much to Richard last year.

'You have got to think of something, Richard,' I said, although I do not always know if he is listening properly. 'I have a feeling they are going to invite us to celebrate Onslow's

birthday. Now, you know I would not want to upset them, but you know what it's going to be like. Bunfight at the O.K. Corral. Daisy's planning to take him to some restaurant for lunch, but if it's Onslow's choice we are going to be knee deep in chips and sauce bottles in the first five minutes.'

But of course, Richard thought of nothing and when the call came through, what could I do but accept? 'Of course, we'd love to come to Onslow's birthday party, Daisy. How kind of you to invite us, dear. I know that Richard will be delighted.' Graciousness costs nothing, even at times of great stress.

The importance of the occasion was transformed, however, by the news that Rose would be bringing her new boyfriend, a Mr Marinopoulos. This sort of news can affect the type of birthday present to be bought. When one is invited to a meal with one's sister's Greek friend, the accompanying birthday present, even when aimed at a tattooed and unshaven brother-in-law, must have some social impact. A fully-fledged shopping expedition, with husband and cheque book, is called for.

I happened to chance upon Elizabeth in her garden as I left the house.

'I'm just off to town. I have some purchases to make. We have an important social occasion tomorrow. We are having a meal with my sister Rose's wealthy gentleman friend. He's calling for us in his limousine.'

'Very stylish,' said Elizabeth, with perhaps not quite enough enthusiasm to qualify as polite.

'He's Greek, you know. It's terrifying how wealthy they are. I expect we will be in for a boring time while he talks about his oil tankers and his offshore funds.'

*Cufflinks? For Onslow? But
he never wears a shirt*

I met Richard in town and we went straight to the best jeweller, where of course I am well-known. 'I'll be with you in a moment, madam,' said the shop assistant, clearly recognizing that an important purchaser had just entered his life.

'No hurry. I'll just browse through your quality items.'

Richard was surprised. 'You never usually buy Onslow anything expensive.'

'Well, he is family, after all,' I said, studying the extensive range of hallmarked silver goblets and salvers in their display cabinet.

'He's been family for a long time. But this is the first occasion he's been in line for something expensive.'

'Richard,' I said with quiet emphasis, 'we shall be quite an intimate little group at luncheon tomorrow. You surely do not imagine that I could present Onslow with something cheap and tawdry in front of Rose's wealthy gentleman friend?'

'Oh, I see,' said Richard. On occasion, he does eventually grasp some of the finer points of etiquette.

'I have my pride.'

'Lucky for Onslow.'

'I thought something expensive, but tasteful. Cufflinks.'

'Cufflinks? For Onslow? But he never wears a shirt.'

Richard misunderstands the basic purpose of birthday presents for those on whom we look down with love from our more exalted social position.

'Precisely,' I said. 'We must encourage him. And a pair of gold cufflinks might do the trick.'

*W*here do family pets fit in with the etiquette of home *life?* asks Mrs Julie Brown from Truro, who has obviously noticed my natural rapport with the animal kingdom.

You cannot leave half a camel
in a private driveway

Well, of course my sister Violet has room for a pony, but has not yet got round actually to owning one, which may be because she has enough trouble mucking out her husband Bruce, without taking on extra equine responsibility. I too love animals and am sure that they are all very well in their place, but their place is not in a house with expensive carpeting and new wallpaper in the lounge.

One of Rose's gentleman callers, Roger I think his name was, once called at our home by mistake, in the company of a very large dog called Olive. Large dogs do not suit our driveway,

so I was forced to ask Roger to remove it.

'Please take that thing out of my driveway.'

'Thing?' said the man, rather shocked. 'I'll have you know this is a pedigree thing.' As if that made things any better. I am not one to be impressed by mere pedigree, in dogs or in people.

'Will you kindly remove it. You cannot leave half a camel in a private driveway, and I'm expecting company any minute.'

'Oh come on, Olive,' said Roger to the dog. 'We'll come back when Rose's mother has gone away.' This is not the sort of comment that endears me to a man, even if he is one of Rose's friends.

But Olive refused to 'come on'. She sat there stolidly in my driveway, sitting stolidly being her only accomplishment, as far as I could see. Roger could not move her, however hard he tried. And that is one of the troubles with dogs, which I never have with Richard. They are not always obedient. And they moult.

Roger dropped Olive's lead and began to walk away.

'Where are you going?' I shouted at his departing back.

'There's a little dog at the end of the road she always plays with in the park. She'll move when she sees him. I'll be back as soon as I can. In the meantime don't feed her.'

'I have no intention of feeding her.' And with that he disappeared, thus proving that Roger was no gentleman, and an entirely unworthy suitor for Rose. Good pet etiquette does not include abandoning large dogs in weedless and recently swept driveways.

Onslow has a dog. It tends to live in the car by what remains of their front gate. It adopted them one day, and spends most of its time terrifying people who walk up the drive, especially people who are tastefully dressed in elegant dresses and floral hats. Perhaps it is the extreme scarcity of anybody smartly dressed which takes him by surprise. Be that as it may, he has done no more than his owner to endear himself to me. When once I had the terrible experience of sharing the back seat of Onslow's car with Rose and Emmet among several others, I sat on the dog's chewed and quite probably regurgitated squeaky toy. As I pulled this unspeakable object from beneath my second-best summer outfit in matching blues, all Onslow could say was, 'Great! That's the dog's. She'll be glad you've found that.' All I can say is I'm pleased that so far she has not had the opportunity to express her appreciation to me.

That large Irish wolfhound (a foreign breed, needless to say) is not the first dog that Onslow has shared a lifestyle with, as I discovered one day when Daddy went out without telling anybody where he was going.

'I think it's terribly careless of you, Daisy, to lose Daddy,' I said.

'Nobody's perfect,' replied my dear sister. In her case, she is quite right, though there are some of us who feel it our duty to strive for perfection.

'You can't keep them in if they want to roam,' said Onslow, ever the philosopher. 'We had a bull terrier who was just the same.'

'I don't think I care for that comparison, Onslow.'

'It cured him when we had him doctored,' he went on.

'Or that one.'

'Well, we had to stop him biting the postwoman.'

We have never had a dog. I can't do with the mess.

CHAPTER THREE

IMPROVING THE MIND

J UST A FEW nights ago, as I lay in bed wearing my genuine silk and polyester mix pink pastel nightdress, I thought I heard a noise.

'I heard a noise,' I said to Richard.

'There's no one there,' replied Richard, with what I considered a cavalier disregard for the possible safety of his loving wife and our many valuables. It did not take me long to appeal to his conscience and persuade him to jump up out of bed, put on his puce Paisley dressing gown with matching slippers, and check that all was still well in our world.

He was back within a few moments. 'There's no one there,' he repeated. 'Everything's locked, bolted, barred.'

'You checked the windows?' I asked. Burglars are very athletic nowadays.

'I checked the windows.'

'What about the garage?'

'Yes, that's still there,' said Richard, taking off his puce Paisley dressing gown and matching slippers and getting back into bed.

'I can't understand really why we've never been burgled. It's common knowledge that I have some very valuable *objets*

Maxwell, Nixon And Kray
Insurance Valuations to the Gentry

Valuation of Goods For Insurance - Mrs. Richard Bucket

ITEM   VALUATION

Imitation Queen Anne Corner Cabinet — *Silly man, can't he tell an*
(as seen in Sandringham House) — *original when he sees one!*
£195.00

Royal Worcester Double Glazed Avignon Crockery
(24 pieces)

4 ~~Imitation~~ Meissen Figurines (circa 1936)   £ 72.00

Set of Royal Doulton cups and saucers with   £ 12.00
hand-painted periwinkles (slightly chipped)

Print of Sutherland portrait of Sir Winston   £ 20.00 — *still good*
Churchill, with gilt frame   *as new,*
                                                                    though!

4 silver plate candlesticks   £ 14.50

Slimline pushbutton telephone with recall facility   £ 30.00 — *they're*
                                                            £ 55.00   *worth much*

8 Photograph albums, containing blurred   *more than*
photos of small child — *these are priceless!*   £ 4.00   *that!*

TOTAL VALUE FOR INSURANCE PURPOSES
                                                            £402.50

Our fee (25% of valuation)
                                                            £100.62

Prompt payment will be most appreciated, dear lady.

Yours faithfully,
for MAXWELL NIXON & KRAY

but it's worth a lot to me

d'art.' I was thinking in particular of my Royal Doulton and the figurines that were Grandmama's. Richard does not seem to place the same value on them as I do, which may be why we have never been burgled. Has word reached the criminal classes that the master of the house does not think his wife's heirlooms are valuable? But how would Richard ever come into contact with the criminal classes? Onslow is unwashed, yes, but not criminal.

'The Wilkinsons were burgled,' I added, as Richard turned out his bedside light and settled down to sleep. 'On his income I can't understand how they could afford to be burgled. Quite honestly in their circumstances I think it's a mite pretentious for them to be burgled.' I have never been able to cope with pretentiousness, but Richard declined to comment. I tried again.

'One day they will be Sheridan's.'

'The Wilkinsons? One day the Wilkinsons will belong to Sheridan?'

'Don't be silly, dear. I mean my *objets d'art*. One day they will be Sheridan's.'

The name Sheridan always brings Richard back to life. He is such a loving father. Nothing is too much trouble for him. He does not have that close psychic link with his son that I, as his mummy, seem to have, but still he feels deeply all that Sheridan does. He sat up in bed and put on what I can only describe as his *paterfamilias* voice. It is not very different from his usual voice, of course; nothing about Richard is ever very different from usual, I am pleased to say.

'I think some time we ought to have a talk about Sheridan.'

'What on earth do you mean, dear?'

'We put him into higher education because you wanted him

to be a Quantity Surveyor.' (My Sheridan is at the Polytechnic which gave him such a good grant to stop him being tempted by Oxford or Cambridge. Quantity surveying is such important work, and you have initials after your name to let everybody know how well qualified you are.) 'So why has he dropped maths in favour of needlework?'

A strange question at three in the morning when one has just been chasing burglars, but I knew the answer.

'Because he's started making all his own clothes.'

Richard would not let the subject drop. 'Don't you ever worry about him?'

Of course I worry about my dear Sheridan, but I also know that his education will stand him in good stead throughout his life. If one is truly to maintain one's position in society, then a fully educated mind is absolutely essential. I should emphasize that a fully educated mind is not necessarily one that knows everything, although my closest friends and family will acknowledge with feeling that there are times when I appear to. A fully educated mind is one that knows what's best.

A fully educated mind will probably have been involved in higher education. My neighbour Elizabeth has a daughter, Gail, who is also in higher education, but she has rather let poor Elizabeth down by concentrating less on her studies and more on living openly with a boy called Harold, of all things. Elizabeth professes not to be disappointed, but she hides life's little trials well. My Sheridan has promised his mummy not to get involved with girls while he is in higher education, and neither he nor his friend Tarquin ever seem to bother with the opposite gender.

But even those of us who have finished with the exam-

passing part of education should know that a full social life obliges us to keep well-informed, and to seek out knowledge wherever it may be. It is not merely a matter of collecting tasteful *objets d'art* to such an extent that the only way to avoid being burgled is to spread false rumours that they are worth very little, it is also essential to educate one's neighbours to appreciate the beauty of one's Royal Doulton and Grandmama's hand-painted periwinkles. Each one is worth forty pounds and is irreplaceable, as I told Elizabeth when she dropped one at the Church Ladies' Buffet Lunch with Guest Speaker.

I now turn, with perfect timing I think you will agree, to another question from a socially eager but insecure member of my public.

Dear Mrs Bucket, she writes, *How can I be sure that I am always correct in my pronunciation and grammar when conversing in public?*

This is a problem for many people. The postman, the milkman and even the Vicar have been known to make the simple mistake of pronouncing our surname the way it is spelt, as Bucket rather than Bouquet. As I explained to the Vicar, the name is of French origin. I believe my husband's family in the distant past were Eugenics or something. Not that there's any French blood in him now, of course. The Vicar is quite safe. There are no French habits here.

But uncertain grammar can strike at any time, and we must

always be vigilant. For example, the other day Richard walked into the house as I was putting the finishing touches to one of my candlelight suppers and called, 'It's only me.'

I carried on for a few moments, but then the error struck me, and I felt obliged to correct him. 'Shouldn't that be, "It's

*The Vicar is quite safe. There are
no French habits here*

only I'', dear? Especially when you're shouting it where the neighbours can hear.'

'I'm not sure,' said Richard, as decisive as ever.

'Neither am I. So you must be careful.'

Then there was the occasion on which my sister Rose, in

It's us women that suffer

the company of the wife of one of her boyfriends, was lamenting the fickleness of the male gender. 'Men,' she said. 'They're all swines.' Through her tears, Rose's boyfriend's wife commented that, 'It's us women that suffer.' I could not help noting that it should have been, 'It's we women who suffer.' How typical of Rose to fall for a man whose wife has not grasped the finer points of a well-turned-out sentence.

*D*ear Hyacinth, asks a correspondent in a more familiar style than is customary amongst those who have yet to go through the formalities of an introduction by a third party, *How important is music in the life of an educated member of society?*

Music is a central part of my life. I remember once when I was flicking dust from the leaves of the rose bushes in my front garden, that dear Emmet was playing his piano next door. 'Listen to that,' I remarked to a man who was passing by. 'Doesn't he play beautifully?'

The man edged away from me. I have often noticed how people seem slightly uncomfortable in my presence, no doubt because of my relentless good taste in all things, but as he backed against a tree, he was able to say 'Yes, he does.'

'Brahms, I think.'

The man rather unexpectedly said, 'Mendelssohn, surely.'

'Just testing,' I laughed gaily at his rapidly departing back.

A moment or two later, Elizabeth emerged onto her front

Book of Etiquette

Music is a central part of my life

doorstep wearing her candlewick dressing gown, which I must admit I consider to be a little scantily dressed for the great outdoors, and with so many degenerates about these days. But after only the briefest of neighbourly remonstrances for her lapse in sartorial elegance, I was able to compliment her on her brother's beautiful piano playing. 'I do love Mendelssohn,' I added.

'It's Chopin, I think,' said Elizabeth.

'Yes, of course. Chopin. Some fool walking past said it was Mendelssohn.' But that reinforced my point about her dressing gown. 'You see, not only degenerates about, but musical ignoramuses.' Or is it ignoramii? Some words are sent to try us.

Dear Mrs Bucket, how can I easily acquire the socially valuable cultural education that is needed if I am to aspire to giving candlelight suppers?

What ignorance this letter displays! The writer will have to learn that no socially valuable cultural education is acquired easily. It is only acquired in a continuing battle against ignorance and prejudice, a struggle that will continue throughout your life or until you feel quite naturally at home with potted bay trees by your front door and the cleanest electricity in the Avenue, whichever is the sooner. I am proud to say I am generally on the winning side in this battle.

However, while it may not be easy to find the enlightenment that all good hostesses need, there are certain steps that can be taken by all of us. A trip in the country is always a source of valuable social information for the inquiring mind. I remember remarking to my next door neighbour one Sunday about this very subject.

'How relaxed and casual you look,' I said to Elizabeth, who could not fail to notice the difference between her less than pristine gardening outfit and my dress, so splendidly offset by my patriotic blue hat and white gloves. 'Perhaps I ought to be gardening too, but Richard insists on taking me for an outing, somewhere educational, naturally – to soak up a little culture. I feel I owe it to Sheridan. I expect I'll become quite an expert in local history and antiquities. I think I'd like that. I could perhaps give a talk occasionally.'

'I'm sure you could talk, Hyacinth,' said Richard loyally. 'I'm absolutely positive you could talk.'

We set off for Carldon Hall, a most imposing stately home within Sunday driving distance of our home, which we visit regularly as part of our duty to be fully versed in local history, but my conscience pricked me and I knew we would have to turn round so that I could visit Daddy on the way. A conscience is such an awkward thing at times, but it is what separates us from the beasts – like Onslow. Daddy was his usual calm self; that is to say, his usual well-sedated self, so we were soon able to set off again on an outing of pure educational pleasure. As I left Daisy's house, I overheard Onslow talking to my Richard.

'Where are you heading for today?' asked my tattooed brother-in-law.

'Hyacinth likes to visit stately homes. We shall probably end up in Carldon Hall.'

'Carldon Hall.' The vast unwashed hands opened another can of lager. 'That sounds like it might be really boring.'

Richard, in an attempt not to show up his brother-in-law, for whom he shows levels of tolerance which are not normally present in a former Deputy Manager of Finance and General Services, merely agreed. 'I expect so. It usually is.'

One can quickly set oneself apart from the paying visitors to Carldon Hall

One of the most pleasant things about Carldon Hall is that we are nearly on intimate terms with the family. I'm not saying I'm family, but I have written to Her Ladyship for charitable purposes. So when we visit, we always go straight to one particular spot in the oak-panelled hall, which is right by a doorway with a sign which reads, PRIVATE – NO PUBLIC ACCESS.

81

A recent audience with Her Majesty

As I have told Richard often enough, one of these days I am going to catch His Lordship's eye, or better yet Her Ladyship's, and I shall strike up an acquaintance. Richard is not so sure. He complains that he has never seen anyone in the private quarters yet, but I have counselled patience.

'The great thing to remember about the aristocracy is their

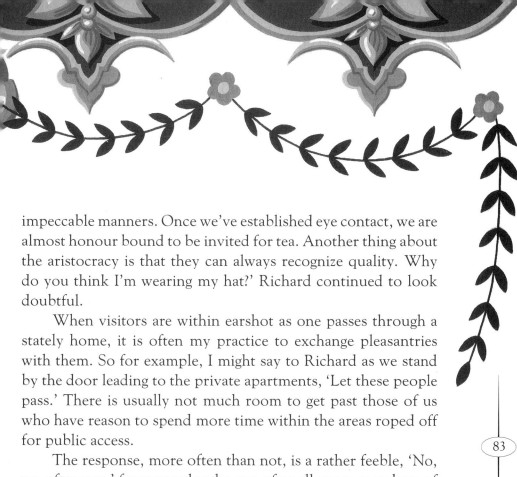

impeccable manners. Once we've established eye contact, we are almost honour bound to be invited for tea. Another thing about the aristocracy is that they can always recognize quality. Why do you think I'm wearing my hat?' Richard continued to look doubtful.

When visitors are within earshot as one passes through a stately home, it is often my practice to exchange pleasantries with them. So for example, I might say to Richard as we stand by the door leading to the private apartments, 'Let these people pass.' There is usually not much room to get past those of us who have reason to spend more time within the areas roped off for public access.

The response, more often than not, is a rather feeble, 'No, no, after you,' from people who are, after all, mere members of the general public.

'It's quite all right, thank you. We are waiting for His Lord-ship.' With a grand gesture I have often practised, rather like a royal wave, one can quickly set oneself apart from the paying visitors to Carldon Hall.

'Oh, I'm sorry. I thought you were . . .' How quickly people become lost for words when confronted by their social superiors!

'Yes, I know. People keep making that mistake.'

As I was remarking to my sister Violet only the other day (you know, the one with a new Mercedes, a sauna and room for a pony), I'm not the sort of person who brags about her social connections, and some carping folk might suggest that we were stretching the truth a little. All the same, the look of respectful awe that comes over these poor people when they

*There is little that can be
done for Onslow*

realize they are in the presence of somebody of social standing is well worth it. It is my duty to spread a little pleasure wherever I go, and that is such a simple way to do it. I like to read between the social lines, but Richard tends just to look at the pictures.

'We ought to move on a bit, Hyacinth,' said Richard, who seemed to have lost interest in the portrait of the sixth Lord Carldon, the present incumbent's great-grandfather. He was beginning to worry about causing an obstruction.

'Don't be impatient, Richard. Absorb the picture.' That is how to gain that socially valuable cultural education my correspondent asks about, after all, and nobody said it would be easy.

'I've been absorbing it for ten minutes.'

'Ten minutes!' I do believe the veil on my hat shook slightly with the force of my surprise. 'These works of art are painted for people to enjoy for ever.'

'It's beginning to feel like forever,' said Richard, in a tone which I would have described as sulky if I did not know him better.

'We'll leave when I've had a glimpse of the family. I wish to begin building up a relationship with Her Ladyship. I am the former Chairperson of the Church Ladies' Auxiliary. I am not without some standing in the community.'

'But they don't know you from Adam,' said Richard, quite clearly not understanding the importance of my social aura.

'Like attracts like. They'll recognize breeding when they see it.'

It was unfortunate that at that point, as a direct result of Richard's good-natured banter at Daddy's home about our educational outing, Daisy, Rose and even Onslow arrived at Carldon Hall to join our party. There is little that can be done for Onslow; his effect on poor Daisy has been total. It is so thoughtless to look as poor as they do. Rose says that it must be wonderful for Daisy to be married to a bum like Onslow, as she can let herself go completely. Daisy might protest, but here for once I must agree with Onslow: it near enough is completely. And I will not be found on stately premises in the company of someone who drinks beer in his undershirt.

It is an easy mistake to make, of course, and we can all learn from our mistakes. In attempting to avoid being associated by the casual bystander with Onslow and his collection of lager cans, Richard and I walked briskly out of the Hall, and turned into a walled garden where an elderly rustic fellow told us that we were no longer in the area open to the general public.

'It's quite all right,' I said, crouching down behind a large stone flower pot to hide from the ever closer tramp of Onslow's unpolished and undisciplined feet. 'I'm a friend of the family's. Her Ladyship and I are old acquaintances. So it would be unwise of you to start getting officious. We are merely hiding from some unacceptable person who is pursuing us. There are such odd people about. I'm sure you understand.'

'I do understand,' the rustic fellow replied. 'Quite well, really.'

As we were driving home from that final visit to Carldon Hall, I had to give vent to my feelings. 'How was I to know that that was His Lordship? He looked like the gardener. He must be very low down the aristocratic scale if he looks like a gardener. I think it's irresponsible. He has no right to look like a gardener.'

What books and paintings should I learn to appreciate in my search for social acceptability?

My dear, broadening the mind involves more than just a list of approved writers and painters. It would be entirely wrong of me to limit your social and cultural horizons by letting you know what I read and appreciate. However, since you have asked, I will admit that my favourite authoress is Dame Barbara Cartland. The fact that she has been honoured by Her Majesty, to whom she has also been a kind of step-aunt-in-law, has nothing to do with the acceptability of her books, of course. But they are innocent, life-affirming and entirely without any untoward biological detail. And short.

Other aristocratic authors are less reliable. Ever since I once read something about Lord Byron, which I do not need to repeat here, I have been wary of members of the nobility who write. Sir Winston Churchill is a safe bet, of course. I have a picture of him on my dining room wall. His books were rather long, but entirely safe to lend, even to one's grandmother.

Art is a different matter. Richard once came home with a library book entitled *The Beginners Guide to Modern Art*. And this when we have a son at university studying Tapestry Design and Advanced Needlework.

Granted I may not know all the technicalities, but nobody could call us beginners. I have a deep natural appreciation of all things artistic.

As Richard will testify, I am an art-lover. We go miles, Richard and I, for a little culture. At least, Richard says it seems like miles. I love going to art exhibitions. When it comes to painting, I do love a good sunset. I like flowers and sunsets, and I always try to keep Richard away from the nudes. And I

don't care for the modern rubbish, but I do like a frame that doesn't gather dust.

Onslow's knowledge of art is limited to the tattoos he displays, which include a heart in a flower on his right upper arm and another riot of red, blue and purple on his left forearm. It is not right that people use their own bodies as a canvas.

My sister Daisy is always reading. It is, of course, the only acceptable way of passing time in the bedroom next to the large and unwashed shape of Onslow, and she has developed a formidable ability to concentrate her mind on the printed page, to the exclusion of everything else. How else could she survive? Daisy reads books of a romantic nature. Occasionally Onslow stirs and takes an interest. My youngest sister Rose, the one with the slight hormone imbalance, once told me of a conversation that took place while she was in Daisy's boudoir attempting to borrow a cigarette to help her forget Mr Crabtree. I am pleased to be able to report that I have never ventured into that bedroom when it has been full of Onslow. It was Rose's action in attempting to borrow a cigarette from the packet by Onslow's side of the bed that provoked him into defensive action. Suddenly the blankets stirred, a hand shot out and grabbed the cigarettes, and then most of Onslow emerged into the light. He sat up in bed and lit himself a cigarette, without offering one to Rose.

'Read me some book, then,' were his first words.

' "I love you," he said, lifting her gently onto the balcony. "Oh Jeremy!" she said.'

'Oh, chuffin' heck,' was Onslow's comment. I don't think he will ever gain employment as a literature critic. Come to think of it, I don't think he will ever gain employment.

'How can you go on reading romantic drivel when you know what men are like?' asked Rose.

'In this book they are terrific,' said Daisy, lifting her eyes from the page. 'Jeremy has hair like golden corn. He's tall and slender. A magnificent figure on a horse.' Daisy and Rose both turned to look at Onslow's hulk as he pulled reflectively on his cigarette. 'So how come I'm still in love with Onslow?'

The object of her desires just grunted. Daisy turned back to her book for a moment.

'What's "limpid"?' she asked, half a page later.

Onslow grunted again. 'What?'

'What's "limpid"? As in, "he gazed into her limpid eyes". L-I-M-P-I-D.'

Jeremy has hair like golden corn.
He's tall and slender. A magnificent figure on a horse

'Limpid eyes?' Onslow stubbed out his cigarette and gave the problem his full attention. 'Almost certainly a disease of the retina. Little scabs on the retina.' Daisy looked at her vast husband with a degree of suspicion. Onslow carried on with his definition. 'You get it from reading too many library books and ignoring close relatives who are dying for a cup of tea.'

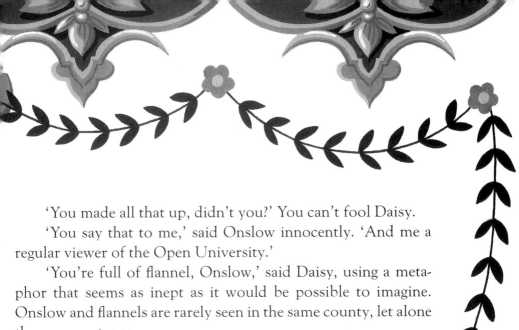

'You made all that up, didn't you?' You can't fool Daisy.

'You say that to me,' said Onslow innocently. 'And me a regular viewer of the Open University.'

'You're full of flannel, Onslow,' said Daisy, using a metaphor that seems as inept as it would be possible to imagine. Onslow and flannels are rarely seen in the same county, let alone the same sentence.

'Ah yes,' replied Onslow proudly. 'But it's educated flannel. Flannel up to degree standard.'

*W*hat attitude should I take towards organized religion? asks one of my more spiritually-concerned correspondents.

Organized religion requires, by definition, somebody to organize it. I am not sure whether our Vicar has the necessary skills, being still a young man, but he has been shy about asking for my help. He need not be. I have a great deal of experience with the Church Ladies' Circle and in charity shops with Mrs Councillor Nugent. I have certain religious quirks, maybe, like being unhappy about garlic on sausages in the church hall, and I am never sure where the church stands on arms as bare as Onslow's. But as I remarked to an evangelist who came to our house recently, 'This is already a Christian household. And I am sure the Lord would have no objection to you remarking on the quality of furnishings you are sometimes privileged to enjoy. My Queen Anne corner cabinet, for instance, is an exact replica

It was a nice christening.
It would have been even nicer if there
had been a wedding first

of one in Sandringham House.'

The nearest our family has come to organized religion recently was when Daisy's daughter Stephanie brought her little baby daughter Kylie to be christened. With Onslow in charge, I cannot say that things ran entirely smoothly, but it was a nice christening. It would have been even nicer if there had been a wedding first but you cannot have everything.

When one of Rose's many admirers proves unfaithful and goes back to his wife, she usually decides to renounce this world. She has threatened to kill herself, but this was prevented by my refusing to allow her to be buried in our poor dead mummy's wedding dress. When Edgar left her, she tried to turn Buddhist, but as I told her, we could not have her chanting mantras. It would wake Daddy.

From the depths of her despair over Mr Helliwell (or was it Mr Bickerstaff?), she decided to become a nun. She appeared in Daisy's front room dressed all in black, with a black hat and black veil.

'How do I look?' she asked.

'Great,' said Onslow, never taking his eyes off the television.

'Fine,' said Daisy, still buried in her library book. Only the dog, sprawled on top of Onslow and his cans of beer, was paying Rose any attention.

Rose stepped forward and turned off the television. Onslow blinked, but it had the desired effect. He looked at Rose. 'Figure in black,' he said. 'I've seen it somewhere. Weren't you in "Frankenstein's House of Horrors"?'

'What are you doing all in black?' asked Daisy, extracting herself briefly from her book.

Religion being organized

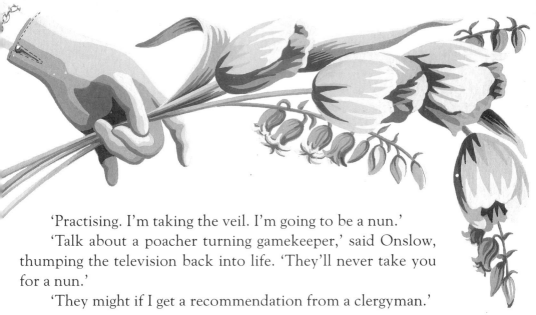

'Practising. I'm taking the veil. I'm going to be a nun.'

'Talk about a poacher turning gamekeeper,' said Onslow, thumping the television back into life. 'They'll never take you for a nun.'

'They might if I get a recommendation from a clergyman.'

I'm taking the veil. I'm going to be a nun

'You don't even know a clergyman,' pointed out Daisy, quite reasonably. None of Rose's relationships seem to have got that far.

'I met that dishy Vicar at our Hyacinth's,' said Rose. I am never sure whether to be pleased or appalled to be referred to as

'our Hyacinth'. Rose has a good heart, of course, especially for one that has been broken every week for the past twenty years, but I do hope that most people do not really assume that I am Rose's in any sense other than the accident of parentage.

'The way you threw yourself at him,' said Daisy, 'he'll never recommend you for a nun. You're too emotional, Rose.'

'I've taken care of that. I've taken a tranquillizer. It should slow me down to a more religious speed.'

'I hope your brakes don't fail in front of that Vicar,' said Onslow, passing Daisy a can of beer to open for him.

But her brakes did fail. She came over to the church hall to find the Vicar just when I had promised that I would sing for a few of the old folk, if Emmet would agree to accompany me on the piano (I thought I'd give them the old favourites. Something classical to begin with, and then finish with something from 'The Sound of Music,' or better still 'Annie Get Your Gun'. Everybody loves my Annie Oakley). By the time Rose turned up, her tranquillizers were taking effect. She staggered into full view of a religious building, and her only excuse was, 'I took a pill. It seems to have gone straight to my knees.'

'I wish we could say the same for your skirt. What are you doing here?'

'I want to be a nun.'

Richard took command. 'We'll have to take her home.'

I took over at once. 'There isn't time. We'll hide her in the church hall until she pulls herself together.'

'Pull myself together? Good grief, our Hyacinth, you're not even satisfied when a person wants to be a nun. How together do you have to get?'

(Top) Everybody loves my Annie Oakley
(Bottom) How together do you have to get?

CHAPTER FOUR

THE PERFECT HOSTESS

I F THERE IS one thing above all that I pride myself on, it is my candlelight suppers. I am sure it would not be boasting to say that after many years, I have now perfected the art of the candlelight supper. For all those who delight in sophisticated conversation in spotless surroundings with the best crockery and cutlery, then my candlelight suppers set the pace.

Some people, of course, will persist in misunderstanding the significance of this style of social gathering, but then Mrs Fortescue has never been my favourite lady, for all that her sister married a baronet.

'I'd love you to attend one of my candlelight suppers, Mrs Fortescue,' I remarked, out of the kindness of my heart to an old lady who probably does not get out very much these days, especially since she lost her driving licence for speeding.

'Candlelight what?' was her rather brusque reply. Richard was driving past a pub at the time, and Mrs Fortescue seemed more interested in stopping for a drink than in the offer of a much prized invitation.

'Suppers,' I said again.

'Have they cut off your electricity?'

Silly woman.

The perfect hostess and some imperfect guests

'I think subdued lighting makes a statement, don't you?'

'I like to see what I'm eating,' she said, showing her innate lack of breeding. 'I'm partially deaf. Be damned if I want to go blind.' With that she relinquished her last chance of ever being invited to the Bucket residence.

Elizabeth, who has had the honour of being invited to more than one of my little soirées, is more enthusiastic in her appreciation of my efforts. 'You will remember, Elizabeth,' I mentioned one bright morning as we were discussing the shortcomings of the postal service, 'you are invited this evening to my candlelight supper.'

'It's engraved on my mind, Hyacinth,' she replied. How sweet.

A successful social occasion begins with the correct form of invitation. It is no good expecting to break new ground in home entertainment, if you invite your guests with an ill-written message on a scrappy piece of paper. A scruffy invitation betokens a scruffy evening. A stiff white cardboard italic printed invitation is the harbinger of a gastronomic and social event that is just too perfect to turn down.

Our invitations are specially printed for us on a heavy white card with an embossed edge. There are so many people who want to share with us the experience of a candlelight supper that we usually have the invitations, with matching self-seal envelope, printed by the gross (if I can be excused using such a word in these days of decimalization). They are sized six inches by four inches (nothing metric will do), and stand well on any mantelpiece.

I do like the use of the word 'cordially'. It is neither too

The harbinger of a
gastronomic and
social event that is
just too perfect to
turn down

Invitation

Major and Mrs Wilton-Smythe

are cordially invited to a

Candlelight Supper

Friday 23rd November
7.30 for 8 pm. Dress informal.

R.S.V.P THE RESIDENCE, BLOSSOM AVENUE

*My best Royal Doulton crockery and crystal glassware with silver cutlery,
laid and waiting for the fully trained supper guest*

formal nor too friendly. It expresses just the right amount of anticipation in the hostess, deriving as it does from the Latin word for 'heart'. It is acceptable for the well-educated recipients of our invitations to know that they come from the heart, and at the same time I find it reassuring to feel that those without the benefit of a classical education will believe that it has something to do with lime juice, and will not expect cans of beer with their meal.

The decision as to who should receive these crisp and embossed invitations is always a difficult one. Some would say that it is important to check first by telephone the availability of one's potential guests, so that one does not have to waste both an expensive invitation card and a first-class stamp on somebody who will have the extraordinary disappointment of having to turn down the invitation when it arrives. I however feel that this is an unnecessary and rather ungenerous precaution to take. Imagine the satisfaction of anybody who receives one of our invitations in the post; it will brighten up their day just to receive it, even if they are unable to accept. And who am I to deny my friends the thrill of displaying such an invitation on the mantelpiece, to show casual visitors that they are worthy to be invited to one of Hyacinth Bucket's candlelight suppers!

The success of the supper depends on three things – the seating arrangements, the cleanliness of my best Royal Doulton crockery and crystal glassware, and the quality of my bathroom linen. Some people, who have coarser skin, are willing to put up with towels which are rather hard and knotty, but if I dried myself on them, I would probably lose an entire layer of my epidermis. I have an unblemished reputation at home for the

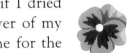

quality of my bathroom linen. It is one of the attractions of my candlelight suppers that our guests are able to take a peek at the quality of my bathroom linen.

The seating arrangements are often the key to the success of the evening. We usually have eight people seated round my elegant and regularly French-polished extendible dining-room table with matching armchairs, and I try very hard not to have to sit next to either Major Wilton-Smythe or Violet's husband Bruce. The Major has a way of conducting himself when in my presence that I do not always find helpful to me in my role as hostess. It is difficult to maintain one's dignity, which is so much a part of my candlelight suppers, if one is continually being referred to as 'my little minx'. In fact, I might go so far as to say that it is a good job that he is a Major. If he was a sergeant, he would not get a foot past the door.

It's a good job he's a Major

Violet's husband Bruce is quite another problem. He has a Mercedes, a sauna and room for a pony, and what is more he has married into our family, so his credentials for an invitation are impeccable. I only wish I could say the same for his dress sense. However, to sit him next to Richard would be to have two men together, and to sit him next to Mrs Councillor Nugent,

for example, would do very little for her re-election prospects if word ever got out. I think Mrs Barker-Finch is the right answer. She is the type of double-barrelled *nouveau riche* personage who needs to be taught the skills involved in sitting next to Bruce for an entire evening.

I like to have Emmet sitting at my right hand, so that we can discuss our shared musical tastes and bring a little *gravitas* to the conversation, which tends to revolve around strapless ball gowns (from both sides of the equation, so to speak) when the Major and Bruce are leading the conversation. Richard is quite helpless in these situations, and I certainly cannot rely on Elizabeth to help. She just sits there quietly sipping her soup, and trying very hard not to spill anything onto our Sights Of Georgian London tablemats, or even worse, onto our regularly shampooed Axminster carpet. Daisy and Onslow, of course, have not been invited yet. Onslow's continued identification with the shirtless ones tends to count against him when I am drawing up my guest list, and I do not think that dear Daisy has a suitable dress in her wardrobe. In fact, I do not think she has any dress in her wardrobe. Come to think of it, I am not even sure she has a wardrobe.

When we have a new guest at our candlelight suppers, I like to place them with their back to the window, facing the fireplace. There they can see my favourite photograph of dear Sheridan, which has pride of place on the mantelpiece. It gives me an opportunity to open out the conversation into the advantages of education and the importance of needlework, not to mention the number of initials a quantity surveyor can print after his name, all of which I feel are subjects of general interest.

· Putting People in Their Place ·

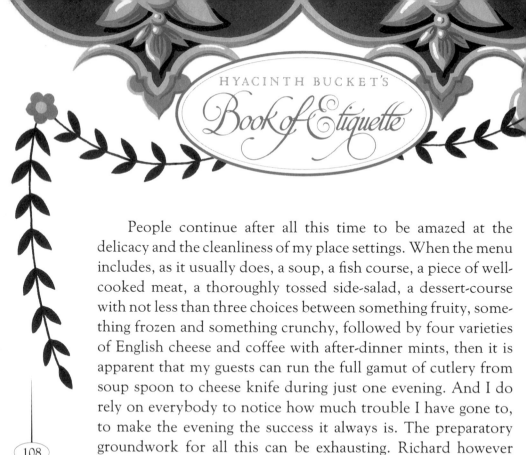

People continue after all this time to be amazed at the delicacy and the cleanliness of my place settings. When the menu includes, as it usually does, a soup, a fish course, a piece of well-cooked meat, a thoroughly tossed side-salad, a dessert-course with not less than three choices between something fruity, something frozen and something crunchy, followed by four varieties of English cheese and coffee with after-dinner mints, then it is apparent that my guests can run the full gamut of cutlery from soup spoon to cheese knife during just one evening. And I do rely on everybody to notice how much trouble I have gone to, to make the evening the success it always is. The preparatory groundwork for all this can be exhausting. Richard however always volunteers to help, and is often to be seen in our walnut-finish kitchen in his apron, happily polishing our silverware under my leadership.

'Don't grunt when you polish, Richard.'

Richard looked up briefly from his buffing.

'I can hear you breathing, dear. I don't think it's quite nice to hear people breathing. You'd think by now evolution would have replaced our unfortunate bodily functions with something a little more tasteful. I suppose it was perfectly adequate for primitive peoples, but really . . .'

Richard continued to breathe. 'Well, we are merely mammals, after all.'

'Richard, what a thing to say to somebody with a solid silver self-cleaning sauce separator.' Richard sometimes says the most unfortunate things, but I have never given up my attempts to train him in how to lead the conversation to suitable subjects. 'Now, I know that this evening is going to be a huge success. I shall use my Royal Worcester double glazed Avignon, of course. I used it last time but nobody noticed. This time, Richard, you will wait for a lapse in the conversation and then you will introduce the topic casually.'

'What topic?' Really, he is so slow on occasion.

'That we are dining from my Royal Worcester double glazed Avignon. I particularly want Emmet to appreciate it.'

'But Emmet's just recovering from a messy divorce. Do you really think he will be overwhelmed by your Royal Worcester double glazed Avignon?'

'He'll find it a great comfort to realize that he's in civilized surroundings, dear.' It is such a comfort to be civilized, I always think. And if a marriage can break up, then Emmet might believe that civilization can too, unless there are people like us willing to show eternal vigilance against the encroaching tide of indelicacy.

Apart from candlelight suppers, what other home entertaining should the perfect hostess perform?

It would, of course, be quite wrong to give the impression that candlelight suppers are all there is to being the perfect hostess. I am also known for the quality of my musical soirées, my tea parties and even for the informal way in which I invite dear Elizabeth round for a cup of tea during the day. As I remarked to Emmet when he first came to stay with his sister, 'Living next door to us, you'll soon learn that you are at the cultural hub of things around here.'

Elizabeth looked worried

I like to think that I am particularly adept at doing things quickly when the occasion cries out for it. I created a cocktail party for Mr Marinopoulos almost overnight. Actually, it was exactly overnight, now I come to think of it. 'I realize it is very short notice,' I said to Elizabeth, over coffee in my kitchen. 'And it will therefore require all my organizational talents. It will be marvellous if you can help me.'

'Well, I'd love to Hyacinth, but I'd planned . . .'

'That's nice, dear. Now I want you to look through my collection of *haute cuisine* cookery books, without of course creasing the pages, and find little things that we can do quickly on sticks. You know the sort of thing. Tasty little morsels of the highest social calibre. Meanwhile, I'll have to see who I can invite here at such short notice.'

Elizabeth looked worried, but she need not have done. I was in command.

'There's you and Emmet, of course.'

'Oh no,' cried Elizabeth. 'I don't know about Emmet. I think he might have some rehearsals tomorrow.'

'He can spare an hour, dear. You wouldn't want him to miss the opportunity of meeting a Greek millionaire. So that's you and Emmet. And I'll ring Mrs Barker-Finch. She won't come of course, but she'll be furious when she finds out what she's missed.' There is much to be gained from inviting people who will not come, quite apart from the saving on gin. 'I wonder about the Major. Oh, just for an hour in broad daylight in a crowded room. I should be safe with the Major. I'll risk it. The Major always adds a little tone. It will make Mr Marinopoulos realize that we may not be millionaires but we do have our standards.'

'Are there any other Greeks coming?' asked Elizabeth, ruffling through my first edition copy of *One Hundred-and-One Things to Do with a Sausage, a Pineapple and a Piece of Cheddar*.

'Oh no, dear,' I replied decisively. 'They break plates. He may have a tanker in every port, but I'm not sacrificing my Royal Doulton with the hand-painted periwinkles.' I used my best piercing gaze on Elizabeth. 'There aren't that many left.'

Book of Etiquette

*Emmet appreciates the trouble I go to, even for
a simple neighbourly morning chat*

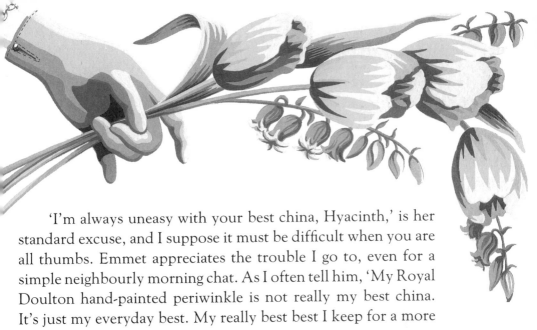

'I'm always uneasy with your best china, Hyacinth,' is her standard excuse, and I suppose it must be difficult when you are all thumbs. Emmet appreciates the trouble I go to, even for a simple neighbourly morning chat. As I often tell him, 'My Royal Doulton hand-painted periwinkle is not really my best china. It's just my everyday best. My really best best I keep for a more formal occasion, such as a musical soirée followed by a little candlelight supper.'

When I invite people round for an informal cup of coffee, whether it be in the morning or the afternoon, I do like them to be prompt. Elizabeth has learnt by now that promptness is a mark of politeness, even if her watch sometimes lets her down. If I say ten forty-five, for example, I do hope people arrive at ten forty-

I'm always uneasy with your best china, Hyacinth

five, and not at ten forty-four or ten forty-six. My coffee is, of course, always the best. An aromatic nut-roasted special is so much more gritty, is it not, than a teaspoonful of instant. My specially prepared Earl Grey with a slice of lemon is much more elegant than a teabag as advertised by chimpanzees.

The Vicar and his wife first called at our house on a Saturday just a very few days after his induction into our parish. I served them with afternoon tea and light refreshments, one step up on the formality scale from mere Earl Grey and biscuits with Elizabeth and Emmet. 'Light refreshments' covers a multitude of sins, much more than mere biscuits, of course, although I found it hard to persuade the Wholesome Bakery of the importance of the order I was placing with them over the telephone. Six superior fresh cream cakes for the Vicar and his wife is an important order in anybody's book, and I cannot understand

Emmet and I sharing an aromatic nut-roasted special
cup of coffee from my everyday best china

why they were so reluctant to deliver. I am afraid that the spirit of service lives on in so few of us nowadays.

As a general rule, it is best to seat vicars on sofas. Possibly Daisy's sofa would be the exception that proves the rule, but I have had many a religious inspiration on our sofa with its regularly dry-cleaned floral loose-fitted covers. With the Vicar and I seated together on the sofa, Christian goodness and sincerity just flows out across our lounge. Vicars' wives sit on chairs. That way they can be in easy reach of my tasty homemade canapés. And Elizabeth sits on whatever chair remains. 'Now then, Elizabeth, if you could pass round my Royal Doulton with hand-painted periwinkles,' I said.

Elizabeth fluffed her lines. 'Oh, must I, Hyacinth? I shall be terrified of dropping one.' Her hands shook and the cup and saucer rattled in her rapidly loosening grip. 'I think it might be better if we all help ourselves.'

'Oh yes,' said the Vicar's wife, displaying an independence of mind I had not credited her with. 'We can all do that.'

I did have in mind something rather more orderly.

I find it very useful to rehearse the main points of any important social function. I never like leaving things to chance. That is the mark of a thoughtful hostess. However, with sisters like mine, it is often difficult to foresee all the emergencies that may arise during the course of afternoon tea and light refreshments, so even a rehearsal with Elizabeth, who will persist in sitting in the wrong chair however often I tell her I like to face the window, cannot always ensure a trouble-free social occasion. When Mrs Henderson was expected for tea, I made a point of asking Elizabeth for her opinion.

'But I'm not really dressed for visiting,' said Elizabeth, clambering over the little wall which divides our gardens, and trotting towards my front door.

'As if that matters between friends,' I replied, showing the caring informality which must be the basis of any good relationship between neighbours. 'Take your shoes off, dear.'

'I'm surprised you want my opinion, Hyacinth,' said Elizabeth as she took off her rather scuffed everyday shoes. 'I seem to go to pieces on these premises.' At least Elizabeth is aware of her own shortcomings.

'Now, I was wondering if I should press Mrs Henderson to take a little light sherry with her light refreshments, or shall I stick to tea?'

'And you really value my opinion?'

'Certainly I do.' If one cannot learn from others, one will never develop any social skills, as I often tell Richard.

'Well, I think, stick to tea.'

'No, you are wrong there. I think sherry.' Elizabeth's opinion is always so useful in helping me make up my mind. 'Now this is the big test,' I said, leading her through the hall towards the kitchen, and covering her eyes. 'As soon as I take my hands away and open this door, give me your honest opinion, Elizabeth.'

I opened the door and released my hands from her eyes. 'You've got the stain out where I spilt the coffee.'

*If one cannot learn from others, one will
never develop any social skills*

'No no. It's the tray. Look at the tray. My little selection of canapés and things to nibble.' My preparations are always more than comprehensive, but it is so useful to have wholehearted support for my efforts.

Elizabeth made no sound, overcome by the utter suitability of every item on the tray.

'Oh, I knew you'd agree, dear. Now come along, you haven't got much time if you are going to make yourself nice for Mrs Henderson. You've got your work cut out, really you have, dear.'

I am very good at inviting people to a social occasion in my home, writes a lady from Bognor Regis, *but I am less expert in getting rid of them at the end of the party. How do you end your little gatherings?*

I am not sure that 'getting rid of them' is the way that I would describe the closing moments of one of our gatherings (which are also never 'little'. You may work on a small scale in Bognor Regis, but we do not do so in our Avenue). All the same, it is essential that people realize that even the most successful of candlelight suppers, or the most life-enhancing of musical soirées, must come to an end before dawn. It is here that firmness pays. As Richard once remarked, 'Let's face it, you are firmer than me,' and while I did wonder whether it should have been 'firmer than I', I certainly agreed with his sentiments. I do have the knack of persuading people to go, even though the party may still seem to be at its height. I follow the old show-business adage (which of course I would have followed even more closely if I had allowed myself to build up a professional reputation as a singer of light classics and favourites from the musicals) of 'keep them shouting for more'. Of course, I do not expect anybody to shout for anything at my candlelight suppers, even when Elizabeth spills her *cocktail de prawn et lettuce* in Bruce's lap, but I do like to feel that my gatherings end before people have exhausted not only all decent conversational gambits, but also the hostess.

Daisy telephones with the awful news

I find that when, for example, guests are so taken by the beauty of my garden that they loiter among my roses, it is worth being subtle. I would suggest saying something like, 'Aren't they lovely? You know, there are some beautiful ones down the Avenue, on the left. You'll see them as you leave.' Not that it always works, unless you include the word 'goodbye' in your small talk, preferably in every sentence.

Sometimes it is necessary to bring things to an abrupt end, and it is here that my skills are particularly well-honed, as they have to be when, for example, Daisy telephones with the awful news that Daddy has run off with a Mrs Clayton, of no social

119

standing whatsoever. We have to act quickly to ensure that such things do not radically affect his pensionable status.

'So glad you could come', is a line I often use on Elizabeth. 'I hope you have enjoyed your coffee.'

'I was just about to.'

'Good. Don't let me detain you. We will see each other a little later.' At this point, a firm push through the door often helps get the message across. 'Goodbye, dear.' And with that the door is shut firmly in the departing guest's face.

A moment later the Westminster chimes rang out again. It was Elizabeth, holding out a half full beaker of coffee.

'Oh, thank you, dear. It matches my set.'

I just caught, 'Hyacinth, it is . . .' before the door shut again.

I don't think Elizabeth even realized I was trying to hurry her away.

I feel quite confident about entertaining at home, writes a very self-assured correspondent, *but what about entertaining elsewhere – in public places? What advice can you give?*

I remember one weekend we borrowed my sister Violet's luxury double glazed holiday cottage complete with patio and built-in barbecue, not to mention the fully fireproofed thatched roof, so it was obvious that we had to invite several of our closest friends to a small function there. The preparations were thorough. Of course, I took our own crystal glassware, because it is well-known I cannot entertain without my crystal glassware.

Daisy and Rose entertaining in public places

What's more, Bruce thinks the height of taste is glassware engraved with naked ladies.

It was very important that Daddy was included in our weekend, but that Onslow was not. However, things do not always work out exactly how they are planned. Rose, to whom I spoke on the telephone to inform her of my desire to invite Daddy, told me later what had gone wrong. 'That was Hyacinth on the phone,' said Rose to Onslow, after I had rung off.

'Tell her we've moved,' said Onslow.

'They've borrowed Violet's cottage and they are having a barbecue.'

'Oh, lovely,' said Daisy, putting aside her latest library book, *Lord Tancred Desires*, and stuffing a pair of discarded tights down the side of the sofa. Out of sight, out of mind.

'Oh no,' muttered her husband, scratching his designerless stubble.

'Don't worry, Onslow,' said Rose. 'I don't think we are invited. She just wants us to take Daddy down.'

'But she didn't actually say we weren't invited,' decided Daisy, who sometimes seems to have inherited some of the same determination that I pride myself on. It was at this point that my plans went awry. 'So we ought to stay with Daddy, then. Daddy's not used to barbecues.'

'He might have trouble with his teeth,' added Rose.

'Exactly,' decided Daisy. 'Onslow, we're going to a barbecue.'

'Well, then we'd better take a bottle of sauce. Your Hyacinth's far too posh to have any decent sauce.'

The first rule of entertaining away from home, therefore, is to make sure you know who you have invited. It became clear that I had invited not only Daddy, not only Daisy, Onslow and Rose, not only Onslow's bottle of sauce, but also Mrs Thing. She is Polish. Her name begins with a handful of letters which would cause any self-respecting Scrabble player to take up bridge, so

she is known as Mrs Thing. Daddy is often in a delicate mental state, and there was a time when he liked to take Mrs Thing everywhere with him, as a kind of human, if extremely foreign, security blanket. This rather upset my original plans, which were to feed Daddy first and get rid of them all before our other guests arrived. Richard misunderstood my motives.

'You can't just throw people out,' he said, laden down with boxes of my crystal glassware he was carrying from the car. 'They may overlap a little.'

'It's not a question of throwing people out, dear. I shall just insist they leave early because of Daddy's bedtime. I know he doesn't usually go to bed at teatime, but they'll have the journey, and he'll be excited.' I like to think I really care about my family, and always have their best interests at heart.

But then Bunty from the Manor House turned up, looking for her gun-shy dog. Bunty is a stocky red-faced lady with all the dress sense of the landed gentry, and many of their social attributes, too. I took immediate control, even though I knew it could adversely affect the preparations for the barbecue.

'Richard, find Bunty's dog.' He did not look enthusiastic. 'I want you to find it, Richard. It's quite important socially.'

'The dog? The dog is important socially? I doubt it, if it's gun-shy.'

Richard will have his little fun. He put down the boxes of crystal glassware and trudged off on this simple errand of canine mercy, muttering to himself something about the countryside supposed to be relaxing. He came back a little later without the dog but with a tramp. Bunty had in the interim consumed almost a complete bottle of Bruce's Scotch whisky, which made her even more red-faced than before. Despite this, she managed to identify the tramp as her husband Dorian. It is astonishing how people who have inherited large houses never seem to have inherited any decent clothes to go with them.

Another thing to be careful of when entertaining away from home is dancing. I have always been suspicious of dancing, which either involves people getting too close to each other for decent conversation, or else playing music so loud that decent conversation is impossible. It soon transpired that whenever Dorian hears a tango, his wild aristocratic sap rises alarmingly. Bunty's legs had gone by then, which meant that Richard had to hold her up, but Dorian persisted in the most unbecoming gyrations as we danced to the sound of Bruce's old wind-up gramophone.

'Oh I say, you're a damn fine filly on the flat,' said Dorian, using a rather vulgar sporting metaphor so beloved of gentleman farmers. 'Let's see how you are over the jumps.'

'I've not done this for years,' I protested. 'You know I really should be unpacking my crystal glassware.'

I am not sure that the conga is the most flattering of dances to be seen performing, but Onslow seemed quite enthusiastic as we emerged from Bruce's cottage just as my family arrived.

'Hallo, Hyacinth,' he said with a smile bigger than any I have seen him with since String Vest won the 3.15 at Haydock some time in 1983. 'All go, this early retirement, eh Dickie?'

'Hyacinth, who is that lady you are dancing with?' asked Daisy.

'Oh, that's Bunty – Dorian's wife. If her legs were working, you'd like Bunty.'

We never did find her dog, though.

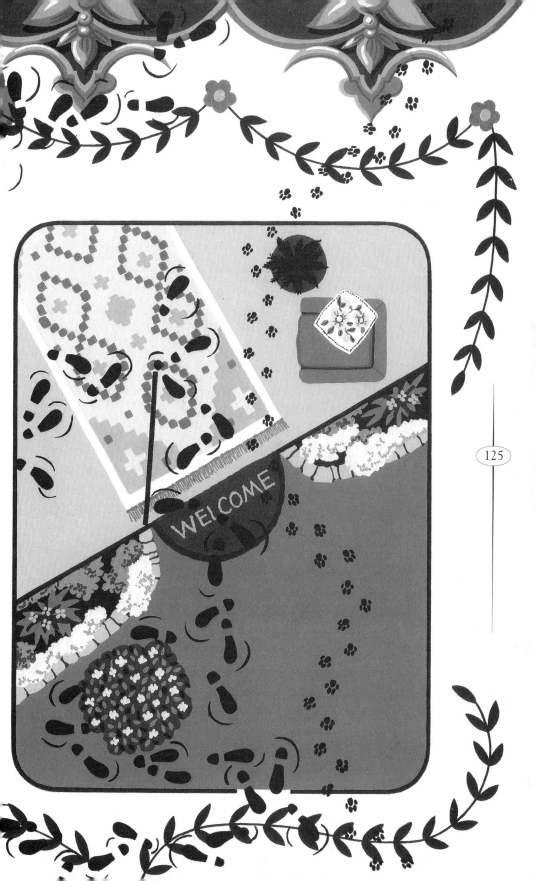

CHAPTER FIVE

SOCIAL OBLIGATIONS

A S I MAY have mentioned before, I expect people to assume that I was born into the candlelight-supper class. But being a person to whom the correct deportment comes naturally at all times does not mean a life of self-centred socializing. We have a responsibility, a duty even, to think of those less likely than ourselves to choose the correct fork with the fish course. We have an obligation to help others. A truly concerned pillar of society these days is not content merely with giving the most talked-about musical soirées in the Avenue; she must also be a caring human being, involved in issues such as The Hole In The Ozone Layer and Church Cleaning. I like to think that I play my part in bringing the attention of my neighbours, especially that snobbish Mrs Barker-Finch, to the good work I do for many causes.

Mrs Councillor Nugent is, of course, someone who shares my concerns. Some may consider her to be rather a severe lady, but we have worked together on many local projects, and I feel we are of like mind in our determination to be seen to help others at whatever cost to ourselves and those we do good to. I remember her saying to me one day as we worked side by side at the charity shop, 'You have to try to bring a little happiness

Book of Etiquette

*A caring human being, involved in issues such as The Hole
In The Ozone Layer and Church Cleaning*

into people's lives.' She let the nobility of these sentiments sink
in for a moment before continuing. 'Not too much, mind you,
or else they start taking it for granted. Next thing you know
they're behaving in a disgusting manner and enjoying excessive
romantic behaviour.' Mrs Councillor Nugent is a force in the
community dedicated to the suppression of excessive romantic
behaviour.

'I won't have it,' she continued wisely. 'There's more to life
than being all dolled up for the opposite sex.'

'Sex? I absolutely agree. I've always warned my Sheridan
against females who flaunt themselves for the opposite sex.' It
does no harm to make people such as Mrs Councillor Nugent
aware that one is not only a caring mother, but also firmly
positioned on the side of righteousness when it comes to immor-
ality amongst the young. And despite the fact that she has been
heard to remark that she has no time for socializing, she often
enjoys afternoon tea at our home.

'Mrs Councillor Nugent is coming to afternoon tea,' I
remarked to Elizabeth one bright September morning. 'You
remember, dear, I told you.'

Elizabeth looked blank. But why else would we be sitting
having morning coffee in the lounge, if it was not to rehearse the
afternoon's events? Sometimes I think I should be working for
Amnesiacs Anonymous. My neighbours would be top of the
list for care and attention.

'She's on the committee for saving something,' I reminded
her. 'Whales, was it? Anyway it is not important, dear. What is
important is that I rather suspect that she is going to invite me
to serve on her committee. And I'd like you to be here, dear.'

Elizabeth continued to look blank. 'Well, that's very kind of you, Hyacinth, but why do you need me?'

'You will be here to make Mrs Councillor Nugent aware of the little things that matter. You know – details that will convince her that I'm just the sort of person she's looking for.' It is

Mrs Councillor Nugent is dedicated to the suppression of excessive romantic behaviour

an obvious but frequently overlooked fact about serving on a committee that one must be elected to the committee first. And that involves hard work. 'Don't overdo it, of course. I'm a great believer in subtlety, as you know.'

'Well, I'll just hover in the background.'

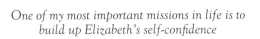

*One of my most important missions in life is to
build up Elizabeth's self-confidence*

Elizabeth does not really appreciate what is involved in getting chosen to serve on committees to save whales (none of which, incidentally, I have ever noticed in Mrs Councillor Nugent's constituency, but it is her affair if she wishes to waste ratepayers' money on matters beyond her immediate area of concern. I suppose it shows a world vision, a phrase I have heard on one of those educational programmes on BBC2).

'But don't lean too close to my ornaments,' I told her. I picked up a delicate Meissen style porcelain figure of a shepherd-ess. 'You know very few people realize how expensive this was. It sometimes worries me. I stand it on the sideboard and still there are people who have no idea how expensive it was. Perhaps you'd like to drop a hint to Mrs Councillor Nugent while I'm out of the room.'

'A hint? You're going out of the room?'

'Only for a moment. While I make the tea. What I want you to do is to take the opportunity of inserting the idea into Mrs Councillor Nugent's mind.'

'I'll get it wrong.' One of my most important missions in life is to build up Elizabeth's self-confidence. For some reason she seems to crumble in the presence of other people.

'You won't get it wrong, dear. All you have to do is offer my services to her committee. Tell her that you think I could be persuaded to serve.'

'Why don't you tell her?'

'Oh no, dear. Oh, I couldn't do that. It might look pushy.'

I have long since come to the conclusion that clothes are the secret of success. I have always, of course, dressed simply but elegantly, preserving an oasis of well-groomed good taste in a jungle of jeans and T-shirts with vulgar messages on both front and back. My dress sense is talked of up and down the Avenue, and my selection of hats is the envy of the entire Church Ladies' Circle. Elizabeth is not always so particular about her clothing, but I suppose that for somebody without any sense of style, nor indeed a body of the right shape to show off a couturier's best efforts, she does reasonably well, poor dear.

'Are you wearing that, dear?' is a question I often ask her in an attempt to put her right.

'What's wrong with it?' is her standard response.

'Oh, nothing, dear. I'm sure it's charming.' Entirely uninteresting, showing no semblance of colour co-ordination, and looking as though it has not been pressed since the day it was bought, but nonetheless, charming enough.

'I – I can change it, if you like.'

'No. No. I couldn't dream of asking you to do that.' One must not hurt people's pride. Sometimes the less well turned-out among us can be very upset by remarks about their appearance, but luckily I am a sensitive soul, always aware of the feelings of others. 'No, I'm sure it looks perfect. How long would it take you to change?'

'Two minutes.'

She soon re-emerged from her front door, wearing a much more suitable dress for dealing with Mrs Councillor Nugent.

'Oh yes. I like that one. I've always liked that one.'

'I've not had it all that long,' said Elizabeth. She is obviously thrilled, in a rather charmingly naive way, by whatever new clothes she manages to afford while her husband is away on business in rather Arabic parts of the world, as she had worn

this particular dress several times before.

'Yes, that's very suitable, dear. You'll blend beautifully into the background.'

At this point Richard presented himself for inspection.

'This suit?'

'Good grief, Richard! Why always ask me? I don't determine what people wear?'

'Do I take it that's a yes?'

'Can't you find a more caring tie?'

You see, clothes are the mirror of the way we feel about ourselves. A smartly turned-out person is someone who feels happy with herself. Or himself I suppose, but when I think of men and clothes, I find my mind drawn horribly towards my brothers-in-law. Violet's Bruce once wanted me to lend him a bikini – as if I would have such a garment in my wardrobe – and Onslow has almost entirely dispensed with clothes altogether. He wears a few ill-fitting and misshapen items as a half-hearted compromise with the laws of indecent exposure, but there is always too much of him on view.

The unceasing quest for a more caring tie

*Onslow can't do with being bundled up
with too many clothes*

'Well, Onslow,' I said to him when once he turned up unannounced on our doorstep. 'Is there anything I can do for you? Lend you one of Richard's pullovers, for example.'

'I can't do with being bundled up with too many clothes,' was his reply. There was no immediate danger of that.

How many rows of pearls should be worn during the normal daily routine? asks a Mrs McDonald from Dumfries.

Well, of course, weather conditions north of the border may affect the amount of jewellery worn, but I must confess that people of our own social standing, Mrs McDonald, tend to feel almost naked without a double row at all times. I find that my favourite blue flowered cotton dress, with my best pearl earrings and a double row of pearls around my neck (not those cheap Japanese cultivated pearls) sets me up for almost anything the day might bring.

I have been spotted occasionally wearing just one row of pearls – for example when I am running the charity shop with Mrs Councillor Nugent. I have a dress which is a blaze of pinks, purples and greys, and which I feel makes a statement to all those who may come into the shop, namely that it was certainly not acquired as a cast-off at a charity shop. With it I like to wear one of my bright pink hats with a blossom and a veil, and just one row of pearls. One does not wish to overstate the fact that a charity shop is the only type of shop in which the shop assistants

(Top) My dress and hat were certainly not acquired at a Charity Shop
(Bottom) My sister Daisy has her own distinctive style of dress

are socially more elevated than their customers, but one row of pearls makes the point well enough. I also always wear a pair of white gloves while in charge at the shop. One never quite knows where the clothes on sale have come from, and there is no point in risking my sensitive skin by touching them. There might even be the chance of my developing some quite unspeakable allergy, thus denying the public my contribution to their welfare while I am confined to my sickbed.

My sister Daisy has her own distinctive style of dress. Despite the fact that her clothes get only about half the wear that more civilized people's do, because she rarely gets out of bed before midday, she still manages to make her outfits look thoroughly lived in. For the christening of her granddaughter she wore quite the most irreligious yellow and black spotted jacket, with a shapeless black and white hat and some yellow beads. Whether they were yellow when she bought them, I have no idea, but they were certainly yellow at the christening. I was in a splendid ensemble of pink and green, with a brooch that made it clear I was the responsible member of the family. Some of us have to keep the flag of finesse flying. But by the end of the christening, I was beginning to hope that I would not be recognized as a member of the family at all.

I am most impressed by the way that your husband is always so well turned-out. What are his secrets?
This most interesting question rather misses the point. The

The raw material from which I create
Richard's dapper appearance

secrets of Richard's dapper appearance are not his. They are mine. Left to himself, I fear that Richard would soon lapse into gardening without a tie, or greeting the Vicar in a pullover. Since his retirement, he has shown a remarkable lack of enthusiasm for his suits, and I almost never catch him brushing his trilby just for the pleasure it gives him. Yet hats are as important for men as they are for ladies. I was discussing a complicated life insurance policy with a young man who came to the door recently, and I told him that once I had checked it all with Sheridan, who as I am sure you will not mind me telling you, is one of the most brilliant minds of his generation and still not too proud to love his Mummy, I would be in touch with him again.

'I did enjoy our little chat,' I told him as he hurried to leave. 'Though I have forgotten most of it, I have to admit. But not to worry. Sheridan will take me through it step by step.' As he rushed away to another appointment, I let him in on the secret of his success with me and concerned mothers like me. 'I do like firms who employ people who wear hats. It's very reassuring to be solicited by a gentleman wearing a hat.' It was not the details of his policy which won me over, nor even the way he took off his shoes in my hallway to expose a pair of black socks with no sign of holes in either foot. It was his hat.

A pillar of the Finance and General Purposes section of the Local Authority

When Richard was still working, as a pillar of the Finance and General Purposes section of the Local Authority, I often used to wonder whether his dress sense was letting him down. Of course, he always wore his hat to work, but perhaps there is more to power dressing than a well-brushed trilby.

'I sometimes wonder about a bow-tie,' I said to Richard as I prepared for our morning kiss before he set out for work.

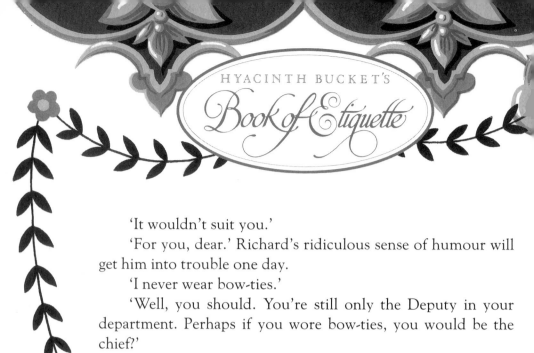

'It wouldn't suit you.'

'For you, dear.' Richard's ridiculous sense of humour will get him into trouble one day.

'I never wear bow-ties.'

'Well, you should. You're still only the Deputy in your department. Perhaps if you wore bow-ties, you would be the chief?'

Richard was hard to convince. 'I don't think the promotion system is based on bow-ties.'

'You are too naive, Richard. These things matter. You'd stand out more with a bow-tie.'

'Especially one that spins round and lights up.'

'Now, don't be silly, dear. You should do it for me and for Sheridan. Sheridan deserves a father full of executive stress wearing a bow-tie. And where's your briefcase?'

'I've nothing to carry.'

'That doesn't matter. You should always look as though you've something to carry. They always promote the people who look as though they've something to carry.' I am of the firm opinion that Richard's failure ever to reach the very loftiest heights of his chosen profession was due to his reluctance to wear a bow-tie or to carry a briefcase.

Since his retirement, I have had to caution him about appearing too free in his style of clothing. Retirement is a serious business, after all. One morning I had to stop him in the hall as he pottered towards the front door with a pair of secateurs in his hand.

'Just a minute. Where are you going, Richard?'

'You wanted the roses deadheading.'

'Aren't we forgetting something?'

'I kissed you good morning. Didn't I kiss you good morning?'

'It's not that. You are not wearing a tie.'

'But I'm only going to deadhead the roses.'

Richard is too free in his style of clothing

There is no such thing as 'only' in my book. 'I will not have you standing out in the street half-dressed. We have a social position to maintain.' Richard seemed reluctant. It was necessary to explain the importance of always looking the part. 'I will not have you out there gardening with your shirt wide open. The next thing you know, you will be looking like Onslow.'

'Sometimes you have to admire Onslow's relaxed attitude to life.' Richard has some very revolutionary thoughts sometimes. We have to be careful not to express them in the open where strangers might overhear.

'Onslow's idea of what to do with a garden is to abandon an old car in it.'

'Onslow enjoys life.'

'Exactly. What kind of irresponsibility is that?'

Daisy still has some vestiges of good taste left after years of marriage to Onslow. Occasionally deep longings resurface from her distant past, but they rarely thrive in the harsh light of reality. When I lent Onslow one of Richard's jackets, which subsequently found its way to my charity shop, of course, Daisy looked at her large and sluggish mate, and said, 'I like you in a jacket, Onslow.'

'What?' said her husband, who has over the years proved himself to be a congenitally taste-free zone. 'This jacket? It's far too small.'

'Any jacket,' said Daisy. 'You look smart.' This was probably stretching the truth beyond its breaking point, but it shows that Daisy still believes there is hope for Onslow. And it must be admitted that any item of clothing which comes with sleeves will make Onslow look smarter than usual.

'You're going broody again.'

'You used to wear a jacket when we were courting.'

Daisy thinks Onslow looks good in a jacket

'Everyone wore a jacket in those days. Even the scruffs wore jackets. That's how you could tell they were scruffs. These days, you can't tell who's a scruff.'

'Our Hyacinth can tell,' said Daisy loyally.

Yes, I can tell. And my list of scruffs begins with Onslow.

Tell me, Mrs Bucket, what sort of destinations are suitable as holiday resorts for the socially concerned?
Taking a holiday is a benchmark of one's social status, and it is therefore very important that the impression is always given that one's holidays are only taken at the most expensive and fashionable places. The main problem with expensive and fashionable places is that they are usually overseas, which means having to mingle with foreigners. The continent in particular is a place where moral decline is a fact of life, so one must be extremely careful not to be seen to be identifying with the continental classes. Violet and Bruce sometimes take holidays in Tenerife, which is abroad somewhere, and look where that has got them. Bruce is a warning to us all of the baleful influence of continental habits.

Delia Wheelwright, that rather snobbish lady who has just added a games room above their garage in Oakdale Avenue, once let it drop in conversation that she and her husband were taking a holiday in the Caribbean. She even had the nerve to ask me to inform the Neighbourhood Watch that they would be away for a whole month. Well, I am not one to shirk my civic duties, but there is absolutely nothing worth stealing in their house, unless a mock-Tudor Inglenook fireplace is worth something on the secondhand market these days, so I saw no point in blocking up the telephone system with a call on behalf of Delia Wheelwright's ego.

'Don't over-indulge on the mangos, Delia,' I told her. And

of course it's full of tourists these days. 'Anyway, happy hols.' Nobody can say I am ungracious in the face of barefaced boasting.

The moment I put down the pearl-white slimline push-button telephone, I began thinking about our own holidays.

'But I thought we'd agreed on no holidays this year?' said Richard, as we walked arm in arm down the High Street a little later that same day. One solution to the holiday problem that we have been known to use is to take no formal holiday at all. This allows one to take weekend breaks in expensive hotels in

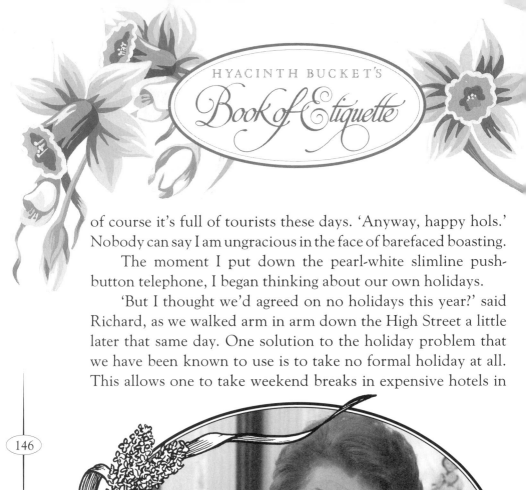

*I began thinking about
our own holidays*

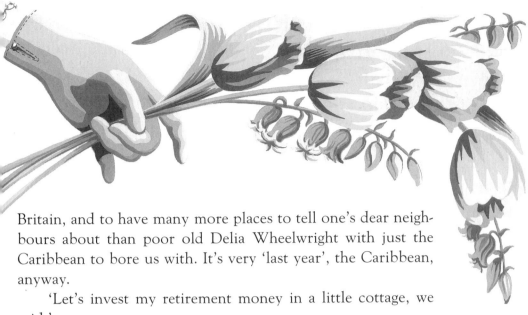

Britain, and to have many more places to tell one's dear neighbours about than poor old Delia Wheelwright with just the Caribbean to bore us with. It's very 'last year', the Caribbean, anyway.

'Let's invest my retirement money in a little cottage, we said.'

A little cottage, like the one Violet and Bruce have, is a wonderful thing, but I am not sure that we could ever decide whether to keep the best crystal at the Avenue or at our holiday cottage. We would be doing so much entertaining from both homes, and I fear that my crystal glassware would not stand the strain of constant journeys between the two.

'When I say, "we said", what I really mean is "you said".' Richard tends to mutter to himself sometimes, but it did not disturb me in my search for the right holiday destination.

I peered through the window of what looked like the smartest travel agent in town. 'I hope these people don't cater exclusively for the spaghetti and chips trade.'

'You're looking for something expensive?' asked Richard, a little line of worry appearing on his brow, beneath the rim of his trilby.

'I'm looking for something very expensive. But we can't go in while nobody's browsing. There's absolutely no point in asking for something very expensive if nobody's listening. We'll come back later when the place is full.'

'Where are we thinking of going that's so expensive?'

'We are not going anywhere,' I said, unfolding my master plan.

'Then why are we going to the travel agency?'

'Because we need brochures. There's absolutely no harm in asking for a few brochures. Very exotic brochures, of course. I'll teach Delia Wheelwright a thing or two.' The secret of the right holiday destination for the socially aware is not that one should actually go there. After all, that costs money and I do not wish to throw away my husband's diligently earned savings on mere passing trifles like a month in the Caribbean. All one should do is let it be known that one is considering going somewhere very smart, and that one could afford it if one wanted to. Furthermore, one can always drop into the conversation the view that tourism is cultural vandalism, and hardly the best way to protect our Ozone Layer.

Mrs Goodbody writes from Burnley, *These days everybody seems to own a car, and as I notice you have quite the cleanest and most sedate of all the cars I have seen on the television, could you please enlighten me on some of the current etiquette of motor travel?*

How clever of you to notice, even through the murk of Burnley, that our car shines like a smile on a clear spring morning. Richard has learned over the years to keep it in fine condition, although I sometimes notice some dirt on the paintwork, especially after a long drive on a rainy day.

Apart from keeping the car clean, husbands are also there to drive. Poor Elizabeth does not have a husband readily available to drive her little car, but in the more well-regulated house-

HYACINTH BUCKET'S
Book of Etiquette

One is considering going somewhere very smart,
and one could afford it if one wanted to

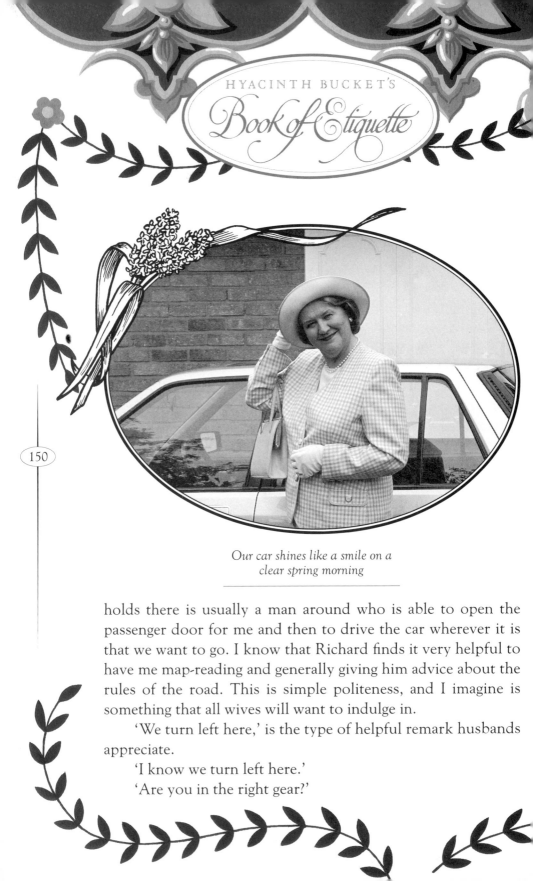

*Our car shines like a smile on a
clear spring morning*

holds there is usually a man around who is able to open the passenger door for me and then to drive the car wherever it is that we want to go. I know that Richard finds it very helpful to have me map-reading and generally giving him advice about the rules of the road. This is simple politeness, and I imagine is something that all wives will want to indulge in.

'We turn left here,' is the type of helpful remark husbands appreciate.

'I know we turn left here.'

'Are you in the right gear?'

'Which would you prefer?'

'Watch the cyclist.'

'I am watching the cyclist.' He then spent too much time watching the cyclist.

'She shouldn't be riding a bicycle with skirts as short as that. Keep your eyes on the road, dear.'

'Well, you just told me to watch the cyclist.'

I don't know what gets into Richard sometimes. It's quite beyond me. I try to ensure his life flows in one placid stream, and yet at the wheel of a car he can become quite tense and argumentative.

'I want you to find Daddy.'

'I take the point, but which way did he go?'

'Well, it's no good asking me, dear. I'm not the driver. You know I never interfere.'

There are times when the car has a social and moral purpose, such as when I was looking for somebody who knows Delia Wheelwright to make sure she would be aware of our holiday plans. Richard did not seem to understand the importance of our mission.

'How long are we going to be driving round and round?' he asked.

'Until I see someone who knows Delia Wheelwright. Try Elm Street.'

'We've just done Elm Street.'

'Now do stop making difficulties, Richard.' Observing the social necessities has never been easy, but we should never let mere geography get in the way of being seen to do the right thing.

We turned into Elm Street.

'Look, there's Mrs Willis,' I cried, triumphantly.

'Now what?'

'Drive on and turn round.'

'I thought you wanted to speak to Mrs Willis?' Richard just does not grasp the subtleties of social intercourse, does he?

'But it has to look like a chance encounter. Drive to the end of the road and turn round before she goes indoors.'

At last Richard was getting into the mood. 'Imagine!' he said. 'If I hadn't taken early retirement, I might have missed all this fun.' He drove sedately to the end of the road, and turned round. He changed gear and the car gathered speed.

'Faster! Faster than this! I want to hear your brakes squeal.'

'You want me to stop?'

'Not yet. I'll tell you when.' We flashed past Mrs Willis working in her front garden (look-

ing remarkably informal, with windswept hair and a rather muddy garden-ing apron), at which point I lightly tossed a couple of brochures out of the car window.

'Stop!' I commanded.

The car screeched to a most satisfying halt in front of Mrs Willis. She was inevi-tably distracted from her most necessary weeding by the

sound of our brakes, so I was able to open the conversation along the lines I had hoped for.

'Oh dear. I'm afraid Richard was driving so fast that my holiday brochures blew out of the window. Have you seen my holiday brochures? You can't miss them, really. There's one about the Orient Express and another about cruises on the QE2. Ah, there they are.' I bent down to pick up the brochures. 'Not a scratch or a crease. It certainly pays to go for the best.' Mission accomplished. Delia Wheelwright would get the message.

Onslow is not somebody who one normally associates with good works. He serves on no committees, rarely invites the Vicar around for tea, and over the years has done little to protect the environment. And yet one morning, he suddenly decided that he should find a cause to champion. The cause he chose was so unsuitable that I have found it difficult to forgive him, but the whole story must be told, to serve as an awful warning to those who would wish to undermine the edifice of social propriety which makes the Avenue the place it is.

Despite the fact that it was way past the time when the more civilized amongst us are having morning coffee and biscuits, Onslow was, as usual, a motionless lump under the bedclothes (so Daisy tells me: I have no intention of witnessing this particular sight at first-hand). Suddenly he sat up and shouted, 'Right!'

'Oh, how strong and masterful we are this morning,' said Daisy, still buried in *His Noble Heart*, a tale of passion in eighteenth-century Cornwall.

'I think it's about time I did something for charity.'

'You certainly know how to flatter a person.'

'I'm serious. It's Richard. Alone, day in, day out with your Hyacinth.' I was not sure how to react when Daisy told me this. When we are together, we are not alone. As usual, Onslow fails to understand how close we are. 'I dreamt about him last night,' he went on. 'I dreamt he was in the clutches of this terrifying monster. Then I woke up and realized it was all true.'

I know dreams are supposed to be symbolic, but I cannot believe that Onslow's subconscious views early retirement as a monster, especially when he himself has embraced the idea from the day he left school.

'All right, Saint Bernard,' said Daisy. 'How are you going to rescue our Richard?'

Daisy and Onslow, using the biological computer to plan charitable works

'I'm still running things through my biological computer.'

'Let's hope you don't have another power failure.'

It was later in the day that Onslow's remarkably feeble plan was put into action. Richard was quietly standing by the car, putting the finishing touches to that day's all-over wax polishing, when Onslow appeared in the Avenue on his bicycle. His bicycle is perhaps the least mechanically-sound machine in the county, but it is significantly smaller than his car, so if he must come to our house, it is better that he does so by bicycle. Richard did not hear him arrive, so engrossed was he in the job he was doing for me. When Onslow tapped him on the shoulder it was therefore no surprise that the poor man leapt a foot into the air.

'Nerves unsteady,' said Onslow. 'I knew it.'

'Well, they're going to be if you're going to do that.' Richard looked shaken, as anybody would when accosted from behind by a tattooed but otherwise shapeless being.

'Have no fear, International Rescue is here,' said Onslow cryptically.

'Rescuing what?'

'Twitchy husbands. You've had a lifetime of being responsible. Now it's time to let a bit of foolishness in.'

'Sounds good,' said Richard, obviously just wanting to humour his large brother-in-law. I know he never meant to commit the indiscretions that later occurred. They were Onslow's fault.

'Let's go.'

'Where to?' asked Richard.

'Wrong answer. Are you really ready for the joys of irresponsibility?'

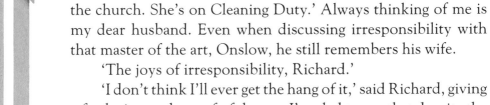

'I think I'm ready. Mind you, I've got to take Hyacinth to the church. She's on Cleaning Duty.' Always thinking of me is my dear husband. Even when discussing irresponsibility with that master of the art, Onslow, he still remembers his wife.

'The joys of irresponsibility, Richard.'

'I don't think I'll ever get the hang of it,' said Richard, giving a final wipe to the roof of the car. I'm glad to say that despite the best professional training that Onslow can give, Richard has never fully forgotten our social responsibilities.

'People think it's easy,' said Onslow, putting his arm round Richard as they set off down the road together. 'Let's give it a try, anyway. What it's a question of mainly is the right attitude and a flair for using one of your plastic cards in your local cash dispenser.' Only Onslow would devise a philosophy of life which depended on using a card-operated public machine for its success. I would never use one of those cash dispensers. You never know what kind of person used it earlier.

The next thing I knew was that when I came out of the house to go to my Church Cleaning (as a small part of my contribution to the welfare of the parish), there was no Richard. It was most extraordinary. I always come out of the house, lock the door, go to the car and Richard opens the car door for me. He had never not been there before.

'I hope I haven't left him somewhere,' I said, as I clambered into Elizabeth's little car to go to church. I need not have worried that my memory was failing. The failing was entirely Onslow's.

It was some time later, as I was completing my religious duties, that Richard and Onslow reappeared. They had clearly been drinking.

'Richard, where have you been?' I asked, showing a wifely concern for one who was lost but now is found.

'Oh, here and there,' said Richard, with a disregard for detail that I find most disconcerting in the consort of a member of Mrs Councillor Nugent's charitable committee.

'Onslow,' I said, realizing in a blinding flash the full significance of Richard's mystery disappearance. 'I hope you haven't been leading him astray.'

'It's only our first attempt,' said Onslow, a broad grin visible through the stubble. 'We got nowhere as far as astray.'

Richard has agreed that there will be no second attempt. Life is too full to help Onslow out with his charitable ideas.

Rose does not understand that legs need not be exposed when cleaning churches

CHAPTER SIX

A HEALTHY MIND IN A HEALTHY BODY

ONE OFTEN HEARS the saying, 'You can't tell a book by the cover.' This is clearly ridiculous, as Daisy borrows all her library books according to the degree of dashing good looks and dangerously tousled hair of the hero portrayed on the cover. What is more, all the publications that Onslow reads have pictures of race-horses on the front, giving a fairly clear picture of what the reader will find inside, always assuming the book is still openable and that the pages have not been moulded together by spilt beer or burnt by a stray cigarette end. You can tell a book by the cover, which is why the cover of this book has a picture of me on the front.

You can also tell a person by her outward appearance, and by that I do not just mean the cut of her clothes. A healthy mind, an active mind which cares about the right way of doing things and the right places to be seen doing those things, will be contained in a healthy body. It is most important that anyone who wishes to be regarded as a leader of local society should be quietly bursting with health. There is, of course, a distinction between bursting with health and glowing with health. Glowing is not a sensible thing to do, as it is usually the result of sporting

activities, which create perspiration. Glowing health is not as decorous as good taste should allow. Glowing is all very well for the shell-suited classes, but not for those of us whose shoes are most definitely not for running in.

W hat sporting activities can one participate in without fear of social repercussions? asks Graham from Colchester.

Well, the first thing to mention, Graham from Colchester, is that I would normally expect to know your surname before entering into correspondence. We must always put up a fight against the encroaching informality of our times. However, this is an important subject that the gentleman from Essex has raised, and I will attempt to answer it.

Swimming is an activity that one can indulge in to fine social effect. My sister Violet has a swimming pool at her home, and of course dear Sheridan has won trophies for swimming. I have in my display cabinet in the lounge the cup that was awarded to Sheridan for doing a width doggie paddle. He was only twelve at the time, although he was very tall for his age. We were holidaying for a fortnight on the Cornish Riviera at the time, I recall.

Daddy has also done some swimming in his time, mainly in the canal. We would all prefer he swam in somewhere more socially acceptable, such as the English Channel or at Violet's, but at least he shows that even at his advanced age, he realizes

HYACINTH BUCKET'S
Book of Etiquette

THE SPORTS AND SOCIAL CLUB
VS
THE REST
on July 8th 1948

INNINGS OF THE REST

Hutton,	b Daddy
Washbrook,	lbw b Da
Mr. D.G. Bradman,	c and b D
Compton,	b Daddy
Mr. W.J. Edrich,	b Daddy
Mr. K.R. Miller,	lbw b D
Mr. T.E. Bailey,	c and b
Evans,	c Richa
Mr. R.R. Lindwall,	b Dadc
Bedser (A.V),	not ou
Laker,	b Dad
Extras	
Total	

INNINGS OF SPORTS A

Daddy,	not c
Richard's Daddy,	st Ev
Onslow's Daddy	not
Extras	
Total	(for

SPORTS AND SOCIAL CLUB WON
NINE WICKETS

MAN OF THE MATCH   DADDY

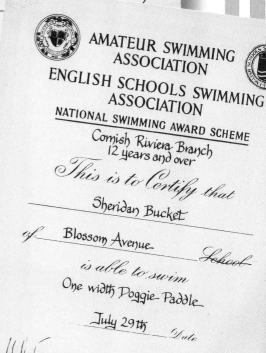

AMATEUR SWIMMING
ASSOCIATION
ENGLISH SCHOOLS SWIMMING
ASSOCIATION
NATIONAL SWIMMING AWARD SCHEME

Cornish Riviera Branch
12 years and over

This is to Certify that

Sheridan Bucket

of Blossom Avenue   School

is able to swim

One width Doggie Paddle

July 29th   Date

A.S.A.

E.S.S.A

fitness is important. In his prime he was secretary of his firm's Sports and Social Club, and a very good slow bowler in his day. Cricket has always been an activity much favoured by the social elite, and was for many years quite sensibly divided into two types, the Gentlemen and the Players. Daddy was every inch the Gentleman, although these days he sometimes appears to forget this proud heritage.

Cycling is another form of exercise that we should look kindly upon. Mrs Councillor Nugent is an ardent supporter of cycling. I met her once at our town's largest department store, where I had gone in order to rescue Daddy from the toy department, where he was enjoying a second childhood. It was not the most opportune moment to come across such a pillar of the community as Mrs Councillor Nugent, but one has a duty to engage in conversation even at the most difficult moments of the day.

I had, through no fault of my own, been obliged to take a lift in Onslow's car to get to the department store, and thus it required both imagination and flair to make the kind of entrance that Mrs Councillor Nugent would have expected from her right-hand lady on the committee. I like to pride myself on possession of both these gifts, and so it was that I commanded Onslow to stop as soon as I spotted Mrs Councillor Nugent outside the store.

'I'll get out this side,' I said to Onslow, and stepped delicately out of his car on the other side of the road from Mrs Councillor Nugent. A taxi had stopped outside the store and was letting out its fare. Showing the sort of initiative that would have earned Richard promotion to Chief of Finance and General

Affairs even without a bow-tie, I crossed the road, opened the taxi door and climbed in. I then immediately opened the other door and stepped out again, onto the pavement in front of Mrs Councillor Nugent.

'Oh, Mrs Councillor Nugent,' I said, showing in my voice

What a versatile form of transport the bicycle is

the restrained surprise that is so necessary when deliberately chancing upon an important acquaintance in the street. 'Thank you, driver.'

'Why are you wasting money on cabs?' demanded Mrs Councillor Nugent, who has a charming way of coming directly to the point.

*You could do the golfing and
I'll be the widow*

'Oh, you know how husbands commandeer the car,' I replied with a shrug of wifely helplessness.

'Damned expensive waste of money,' said Mrs Councillor Nugent, referring I believe to taxis rather than husbands. 'I have a bicycle. I believe in the therapeutic value of a bicycle.' And how right she is, as usual.

'My son Sheridan was a keen cyclist,' I said, once again grateful for the fullness of Sheridan's life which allows me to come up with an appropriate anecdote for all occasions. 'It's partly to that, that we attribute his brilliant mind.'

Onslow rides a bicycle, too. This shows, if nothing else, what a versatile form of transport the bicycle is.

The most socially acceptable athletic pursuit of all is golf, which in all the best circles is pronounced 'goff'. It requires almost no fitness whatsoever and only a smattering of skill, and it gives many wives a pretext for getting their husbands out from under their feet for a few hours. That is why becoming a member of the Golf Club is the very pinnacle of social glory. Richard does not understand this, unfortunately. When the Major and his wife invited us to spend the weekend at Chesford Grange Golfing Hotel, Richard was unenthusiastic.

'It's so long since I played golf,' he remarked rather wistfully as we pulled into the drive of Chesford Grange.

'I hope you're not going to let the Major down. It was very kind of the Major and his wife to suggest that we join them for the weekend. It means that we are socially upwardly mobile, dear.'

'Until he sees how I play golf.'

'Haven't you been practising?' I noticed the Major's little

two-seater parked by the side of the hotel. My first proper look at the hotel confirmed all my best hopes. It was more a baronial manor than a hotel. I knew I would be at home there.

'I don't like golf,' said Richard.

'Now don't be silly, dear,' I replied. It is quite unforgivable of any man married to a lady of substance such as myself to admit to not liking golf. 'You'll enjoy playing with the Major.'

'I must remember that.' Richard has a rebellious streak in him that is most unbecoming in a man of his status. He parked the car and a porter came promptly to carry our bags into the hotel.

While a husband enjoys himself among the eagles and brassies of the golf course (all socially acceptable sporting activities have their own obscure vocabulary which can take many months to master: I think I have the golfing terminology well under control now), the wife becomes a golfing widow. This is not such a hardship, as there are many cultural options at a place as well-appointed as Chesford Grange, and I said as much to Richard.

'I shall lounge and luxuriate and read my Dame Barbara Cartland.'

'If I might suggest one option,' he said, as we waited to check in, 'you could do the golfing and I'll be the widow.'

I took no notice of Richard's unnecessarily frivolous remark. I turned away and looked into the hotel lounge. An elderly couple were sitting quietly taking morning coffee and biscuits and reading their newspapers.

'Oh, this is fine. These people look just our sort.'

Richard looked up from the reception desk. 'How can you tell?'

*The blame must be laid at the
door of the Major*

'They are reading full-sized newspapers. I would never strike up a conversation with anyone who reads the tabloids.'

The weekend did not quite go according to plan, but one cannot put the blame for this on the game of golf itself. The largest part of the blame must be laid at the door of the Major, who not only did not bring his wife with him as he had originally intimated, but also failed to play golf with Richard, relying instead on Porky Hooton to deputize for him.

'I'm afraid it's this damned dicky leg,' he told Richard, who had gone to the Major's room with his golf clubs with all the

enthusiasm of a French aristocrat going to the guillotine. 'There's still some poxy foreign lead in it somewhere. Plays me up occasionally.'

'Listen, I'm not really bothered about the golf,' said Richard weakly. He has absolutely no idea about how social ladders are climbed.

'Not bothered?' The Major may have many failings, but underestimating the importance of a round of golf with Porky Hooton is not one of them. 'Good God, man. Don't say that out loud around here. No, you'll enjoy it with old Porky. Take a hip flask with you. He likes a partner to have a hip flask. Off you go. Porky's waiting.'

When Richard reported this new development to me in the privacy of our suite, he was not a happy husband.

'The Major's booked me in with some complete stranger. Somebody called Porky Hooton.'

'Porky Hooton? Oh, that's very public school. Porky Hooton! You must wear something striking to make an impression.'

Richard adopted his little boy lost look, as if to ask my help in choosing the right golfing outfit. The main reason why golf is so much more satisfactory than all other forms of social exercise is that there does not seem to be any proper uniform. One does not have to wear whites, or nylon shorts and striped shirts with advertizing across the midriff, or even lifejackets and sou'westers as sailors always seem to do. One has the opportunity to impress with the quality and simplicity of one's outfit. This is something that I understand instinctively. Richard is less able to get it right every time.

'I'll advise you on what to wear, dear. This man is probably closely connected with the aristocracy. He may even have a title. They do, you know, with names like Porky Hooton. The one thing they cannot bear is timidity. You must make every effort to stun him with your personality.'

Perhaps it was for the best that Richard never actually played his round of golf with Porky Hooton. The unmentionable behaviour of the Major in his two-seater, when he compared me to the Governor's wife, who was built to last but he loved her, created a need to bring the weekend to a premature but still dignified end, so Richard never teed off with Porky Hooton. But the point is still well-made. Golf is the perfect sporting activity, creating plenty of opportunity for social advancement, without causing more perspiration than is absolutely necessary.

169

*W*hat hobbies can be made to fit in with a hectic social schedule? is a question asked by several correspondents. And there are several answers. One might most simply say that a person with such a full diary as myself really has no time for hobbies, although I love my social round so much that it could be described as a hobby as much as a lifetime's commitment to all that is proper.

But when it comes to husbands, it is important that they have a hobby, especially husbands who have been hand-picked for early retirement. I believe Richard's favourite hobby is gardening. It is one I most thoroughly approve of: in the appreciation

Richard has made a very good job of my garden,
keeping nature at bay

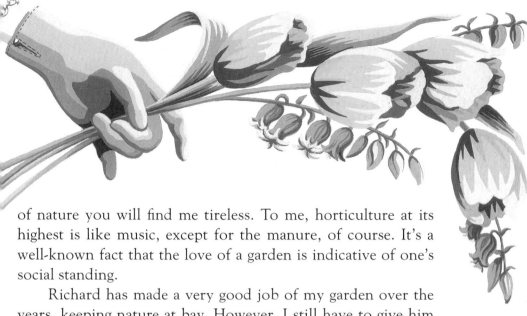

of nature you will find me tireless. To me, horticulture at its highest is like music, except for the manure, of course. It's a well-known fact that the love of a garden is indicative of one's social standing.

Richard has made a very good job of my garden over the years, keeping nature at bay. However, I still have to give him words of encouragement from time to time, to show that his is a hobby we share.

'Are you finished, Richard?' I asked him one morning at the end of breakfast. Richard was sitting at the kitchen table, with his back to the window as he knows how I like to sit facing the sunshine, and reading the morning paper in a desultory sort of a way. He made no immediate reply, so I picked up his coffee cup and saucer and committed them to the washing up.

'I thought I'd just have a few minutes with the morning paper,'

Reading the morning paper in a desultory sort of way

he said, showing that lack of urgency which so many men of his age seem to display. 'Not much point in being early retired if you can't find time for a few minutes with the morning paper.'

This type of statement is the thin end of the wedge. Soon, a man who professes a desire to 'find time for a few minutes with the morning paper' will be laying in bed at all hours like

Onslow. Or worse still, he will turn to the racing pages of these papers and become a member of the betting classes. A devoted wife's duty is clear. She must do all in her power to prevent the slippery slide into inactivity.

'Off you go then,' I said, removing the newspaper from his grasp and wiping the table in a significant manner. 'Into your garden.'

'Not the garden,' said Richard, with an expression that I might have described as reluctance if I did not know him better.

'There must be something out there that needs doing.' It was a bright spring morning, and everybody knows that nature chooses the springtime to produce all sorts of new growths which have to be inspected and improved upon if an orderly garden is to be maintained.

'Not unless you want me to polish it. I've obliterated every weed.'

'There is no need to take that tone with me, Richard. I hope that now you've got all this leisure, you're not going to waste your time being belligerent and argumentative.' Richard looked a little crestfallen, but this is what the experts call 'tough love', I believe. One sometimes has to appear a little harsh, but it is for their own good. Richard's hobbies are his link with the real world, and he must at all times be encouraged not to let his interest slip.

Gardening is an outdoor activity, one in which one can be all too easily entirely visible to one's neighbours or indeed any old passer-by, so it is important that one retains one's standards at all times. I sometimes have to remonstrate with Richard if he appears too casual in his approach. I have even caught him

stretching his arms in full public view after a bout of digging the front flowerbeds.

'I wish you wouldn't raise your arms like that, Richard. Not when you are overheated. It's very common out of doors.'

'It's warm work, Hyacinth,' was his only justification.

'If you have to perspire, I wish you'd go into the back garden, so as not to disturb people who respect us socially.' He has no idea of the embarrassment he could cause if he were found in a state exceeding socially acceptable levels of body heat in the front garden. 'And why are my roses not as big as those next door?'

'They are a different variety.'

'I don't like our roses not being as big as those next door. Are you neglecting them, Richard? How disappointing that you should be neglecting my roses. I want everyone to be greeted by a blaze of petalled glory.' A garden is for all the world to share in, and to appreciate that the size of the blooms by the front gate is probably in direct relationship to the value of the heirlooms on permanent display inside the house.

'This type only grow to this size, Hyacinth,' Richard insisted.

'I'm sure they'd grow bigger if you tried harder.' It is a universal truth in the best social circles that anything is possible if you try hard enough. 'I keep thinking you are out here growing huge roses, and all the time I suppose you're gossiping with passers-by.' Hobbies are not merely for enjoyment, they are to show commitment, and for his own good I try to keep topping up Richard's commitment levels all the time.

'My goodness! Who would have believed it? Is that a dead

leaf? Why are you keeping old dead leaves?' But Richard wasn't listening. He was waving to a rather plainly-dressed woman who was walking down the Avenue. He was still wearing his gardening gloves, which bore clearly visible traces of earth and dead rose petals.

'Richard,' I said, looking up from his store of dead leaves. 'I will not have you waving in dirty gardening gloves.'

'But they get dirty when you are gardening,' said Richard, always ready with an excuse for his lack of proper preparation.

'Can't you keep one pair for gardening and one pair for waving?' This type of planning comes as second nature to those who would never wish to insult a passer-by, even one as plainly-dressed as the person whom Richard was greeting, by gesticulating at them with dirty gloves. The sight of the lady scampering away into the distance confirmed my view that Richard's unclean gloves are a most offputting sight, especially when contrasted with my appearance next to him in a subtle mix of reds and blues and, of course, spotless white gloves. Perhaps in future I will do Richard's waving for him. I am sure it will have a quite different effect.

What is the correct etiquette when plans must be changed because of illness? writes Mrs Diana Chester of Kensington.

Living in Kensington, Mrs Chester, I must assume that you have the correct levels of medical cover, to allow you to be ill at

*I don't like our roses not being
as big as those next door*

times to suit your own social diary. Even living in the Avenue, we manage to confine our diseases to moments when they cause the least disruption, but perhaps it is to the illnesses of others that you refer. The illnesses of others can be most inconvenient.

It is right that we care about those who are afflicted with medical complaints, but we cannot allow contact with other people's germs to jeopardize a very hectic and important social calendar. One must temper concern for the sick with concern for the healthy, who would not wish to be deprived of an exciting evening just because of a temporary incapacity. When Daddy was taken to hospital that time when he so bravely attempted to save the life of the milkwoman by shedding his clothes and diving into the canal, my first concern was for my friends.

'Daddy – ill?' I cried in pain and shock as Daisy gave me the awful news over the telephone. 'How ill? Is it of a severity necessary to cancel my candlelight supper?' I am not ashamed of this: my heart belongs to Daddy, of course, but he is a brave battler against a myriad of confusing complaints with unspellable names, and he can cope without me by his bedside all the time. I am not so sure about my social acquaintances. How would they react to the news that one of my gatherings had been cancelled? I am pleased to report that the candlelight supper went ahead, and also that Daddy eventually made some sort of recovery from his unexpected swim.

One cannot be too careful in guarding against threats of illness. Uncleanliness is everywhere, and we know from medical research how many diseases are spread by wanton disregard for the most basic precautions. Even letters can cause problems, as I was remarking to our new postman – the one who routinely fails to deliver Sheridan's letters. He seems to see nothing wrong in mixing up in his sack all the letters for everybody in the Avenue, including those awful Barker-Finches at number 23.

As I came out of the front door to meet him, he was rummaging through a pile of letters in his sack. He produced one from somewhere in the middle of this pile (why are our letters not put automatically on top? It would save so much bother each morning), and held it out.

*The one who routinely fails to
deliver Sheridan's letters*

'Is that for me?' I asked.

'It says Bucket on the envelope,' came the surly fellow's reply.

'It's Bouquet. The accent is on the second syllable.' They don't train postmen these days in even the most basic skills.

'Well, it's for this address,' he said, and handed it over to me.

As is my wont, I inspected the envelope at arm's length.

'What's wrong now?' asked the postman. I have struck his name off my list of recipients of Christmas boxes. There can be no risk in doing this as his standard of service cannot get worse.

177

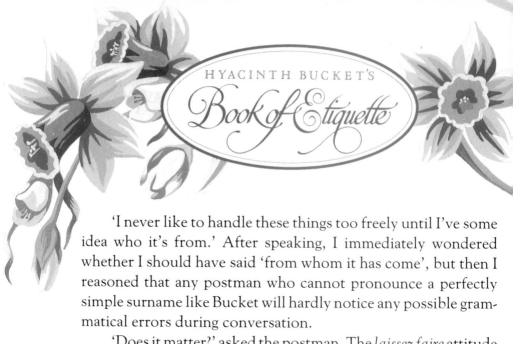

'I never like to handle these things too freely until I've some idea who it's from.' After speaking, I immediately wondered whether I should have said 'from whom it has come', but then I reasoned that any postman who cannot pronounce a perfectly simple surname like Bucket will hardly notice any possible grammatical errors during conversation.

'Does it matter?' asked the postman. The *laissez faire* attitude of the working-classes these days is quite appalling.

'It matters enormously. Some total stranger may have licked this envelope, not to mention this stamp. There may be some prepared to gamble with their health, but I think a certain reserve is called for against the tongues of strangers.' I have never had a day's illness that has been directly attributable to an uninspected letter, which shows that my vigilance has been worthwhile. Although how my sister Rose has stayed so fit, seeing the way she deals so recklessly with the tongues of strangers, is something I cannot understand. I suppose she has built up her own immunity from constant exposure to the threat, like milkmaids becoming immune to cowpox in the eighteenth century.

There is one exception to the basic rule that illness should be limited to the less hectic weeks of the diary. That is the tragic case of the illness of a child. Even the most brilliant child, like my Sheridan for example, will from time to time during his formative years suffer those childhood diseases to which we are all prey, and a mother's place is by his side throughout this ghastly time. When young Sheridan had measles when he was but a baby of nine, I found the whole thing most difficult. Despite Richard's protestations we even went so far as to cancel an afternoon tea and canapés with the Vice-Chairperson of the

*How my sister Rose has stayed so fit is
something I cannot understand*

Ladies' Auxiliary Group. When one has such a close psychic link with a beloved child who is ravaged by a cruel disease, it is impossible to show off one's Royal Doulton to the best effect. Although Sheridan made a complete recovery, apart from one slight pockmark scar on his little tummy, the strain of that time remains with me to this day.

Some people do not trust doctors, but there I must disagree. It is always correct to recommend that someone seek medical advice, in a truly caring way of course, if you feel that their condition is letting them down at the highest social levels. My neighbour Elizabeth falls into this category. She does tend to break things or at the very least to spill things on my best kitchen tiles, and I am certain this is purely a nervous disorder. Perhaps she is allergic to something. A doctor would soon sort it out, or at least give it a good medical name which would sound more important than just being labelled downright clumsy. She says she does not need a doctor, but I feel it might be a bit quicker than my mopping up all the time.

Dear Mrs Bucket, what is your philosophy of life? How do you summon up those endless reserves of energy that are needed to retain your position on the social high-ground?

Ah-ha, the sixty-four thousand dollar question! And of course, being such an important question, there is no simple answer. Perhaps the best way to answer it is to ask other people what their philosophy of life is, and in noting the differences

between their lifestyle and mine, one can begin to work out some of the fundamental rules that I have always applied to myself. And to Richard too, it goes without saying.

Let us start with Onslow, if only to get him out of the way as quickly as is humanly possible. Onslow normally reserves his thinking for the horses, but sometimes the wider implications of the world at large seep into his consciousness. When Richard was supposed to be playing golf with Porky Hooton at that most exclusive Chesford Grange hotel I was mentioning a little earlier, it turned out that unbeknownst to us, Onslow and Daisy came to the hotel to pick up Rose who had been staying there with a friend. (I will not bore you with the details of how Rose and her friend stayed all weekend in room 210 under the pseudonym of Mr and Mrs Smith, and subjected the residents of the same floor to a continuous cacophony of sounds of wanton enjoyment, which is certainly not what hotels are for. If I had known who it was, I would have taken Rose and her friend in hand much earlier. But how can you give somebody a disapproving look if you don't know who they are?)

Anyway, Onslow had turned up, as usual, hardly dressed for the occasion. In fact, he had turned up, as usual, hardly dressed. But the sheer splendour of this type of hotel, which Richard and I take in our stride, made Onslow wonder whether he should have made some nominal attempt to smarten himself up. Daisy reported his words to me, in tones of awe that she should have married such a deep-thinking man.

'This kind of place makes you think maybe you should have a shave,' said Onslow as he steered his car up the drive.

'You should,' said Daisy, remembering fondly the slim and

clean-cut youth she had fallen for all those years ago. 'I think you should have had a shave.'

'On the other hand,' said Onslow, warming to his theme, 'the thing is to act naturally. Be yourself. Always be yourself. If people can't penetrate unimportant surface issues, they're never going to appreciate your fundamental qualities anyway.'

This is oh so true, even coming as it did from the mouth of Onslow. I was astonished to discover he had an awareness of these basic facts of social etiquette, but in his case there is one basic flaw in his argument. Who wants to be yourself, when yourself is something like Onslow? In his case, the only way forward is to be somebody else entirely. It did not take long for Daisy to point out the flaws in his argument.

'What fundamental qualities?' she asked.

'I'm calm in a crisis,' said Onslow. 'That's a fundamental quality.'

'Only because you're too bone idle to rush around in a panic,' said his long-suffering wife.

Bone idle, unshaven, tattooed and only sketchily dressed at the best of times, Onslow still wants to be himself. There are black sheep in the best regulated families, but sometimes when I look at Onslow I have real worries about the future of the human race.

I asked the Vicar for his philosophy of life, because he, as a Man of the Church, must have some ideas on how to behave when, for example, somebody gives only a twenty-pence piece to the Sunday collection. A person who can afford a good hat for church can afford to give more than that, even to a really unworthy cause like the Mission to Unmarried Grandmothers

Be yourself. Always be yourself

(Above) Rose showing her love for all men

*(Right) Onslow loving my neighbour
Elizabeth, who for reasons I need not go into
here, is dressed as Father Christmas*

and Retired Inner-city Muggers.

The Vicar was working in the vestry on his next sermon at the time. He paced up and down, consulting his notes as he did so. 'The point about "Love thy Neighbour" is the question it immediately gives rise to, namely, who is thy neighbour? Thy neighbour is everyone. We can exclude no one. The exclusion of a single person brings the whole concept tumbling down.'

He looked surprised to see me, as though I had penetrated some inner sanctum wherein he could express his rather revolutionary thoughts on neighbours without being overheard. Maybe it was my expression as I took in the full implication of his draft sermon. Maybe it was just that he suddenly realized that he had misinterpreted the scriptures. Anyway, he stopped short, gave a little yelp and said, 'Love thy Neighbour' with some feeling. Then he tossed his notes aside and said, 'No, I think I'll do the water into wine.'

Loving one's neighbours, to the exclusion of no one, is quite clearly an unworkable idea and I am glad that the Vicar has seen his mistake so early in his ministry. It would be awful to have got to middle-age, say, loving everybody equally regardless of their social position.

But some neighbours are better than others. Dear Elizabeth qualifies as a neighbour I am prepared to think fondly of, if not quite to love, which is such a messy emotion, don't you think? Her philosophy is clear. Try very hard not to break any more of Hyacinth's precious teacups with hand-painted periwinkles, left to her personally in the will of her late Grandmama. If one can go through life without breaking too much, then it has not been a completely wasted existence. I once overheard her saying at one of our candlelight suppers, as I came back into the dining-room from the kitchen where Richard was doing the drying-up, that the trick is just to let things wash over you (which in the case of her tea in my kitchen, happens very often). 'I think that's how Richard survives,' she added, rather mysteriously.

Her brother Emmet is rather more Bohemian in his outlook. As befits a musician, he has his own way of doing things which sometimes borders on the unnecessary. Why, for example, does he hold auditions for all the best parts in his little musical productions, when he knows that the Avenue's leading soprano lives right next door? He is not good with personal relationships, though, as his recent very disorganized divorce will testify. He often draws very odd conclusions from perfectly normal every-day events. He described one of my cocktail parties, with three types of wine and just a few little snacks on a stick, as 'a piece of pure scientific research. Good grief, Liz,' he went on, addressing his sister by the rather vulgar abbreviated version of her name, 'If Richard can put up with her, it ... it means that man is indestructible. There are no limits to his power of endurance.' I am not sure which lady Emmet was referring to, and Richard was rather evasive when I broached the subject later in the day, but certainly Richard does not express himself forcefully enough in the presence of difficult women, many of whom I have come across in my long and eventful lifetime in society. Whether his stoicism proves that mankind is indestructible, I am less certain, but Emmet could be right.

Violet and Bruce have no philosophy. Violet complains about Bruce, but he provides her with her own Mercedes, not to mention the sauna, and room for a pony, so I feel she should

Rose loving my neighbour Emmet

*Keeping up appearances is not the most important thing
in my life. It is the only thing in my life*

take the rough with the smooth. 'I know it's a harsh world,' I told her on my pearl-white slimline telephone with the push buttons and redial facility, 'but there are far worse things than your husband dancing on restaurant tables with his hair in a bun.'

My youngest sister Rose has taken the Vicar's concept of 'Love thy Neighbour' to an intemperate extreme, and has even taken to trying to love my neighbour, Emmet. It is a philosophy of a sort, I suppose, but I cannot believe any good will come to somebody who is still wearing last night's little black outfit at nine-thirty in the morning. It is time she settled down, with Boris. Or Mr Blenkinsop. Or Mr Bartholomew or Reg or Edgar or Dennis or Mr Finchley or Mr Helliwell or Mr Butterfield or Mr Marinopoulos or Mr Hepplewhite. Or even Mr Bickerstaff. But I fear that anybody who paints her nails to take a telephone call will find it hard to settle to a life as a wife and mother, however well-established socially her future husband might be.

And my philosophy? As the eldest sister in a family whose members occupy all points on the social compass, I know my responsibilities. Keeping up appearances is not the most important thing in my life. It is the only thing in my life. Oh, apart from Sheridan.

Fin

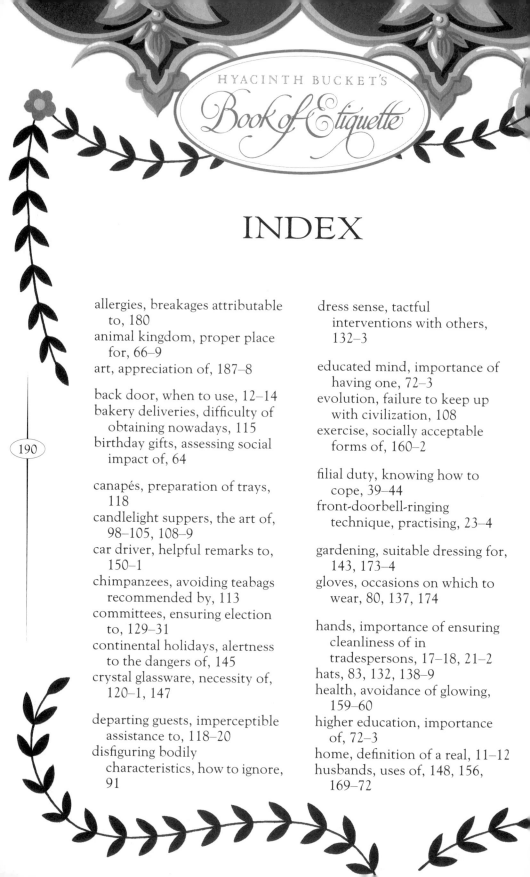

INDEX

allergies, breakages attributable to, 180

animal kingdom, proper place for, 66–9

art, appreciation of, 187–8

back door, when to use, 12–14

bakery deliveries, difficulty of obtaining nowadays, 115

birthday gifts, assessing social impact of, 64

canapés, preparation of trays, 118

candlelight suppers, the art of, 98–105, 108–9

car driver, helpful remarks to, 150–1

chimpanzees, avoiding teabags recommended by, 113

committees, ensuring election to, 129–31

continental holidays, alertness to the dangers of, 145

crystal glassware, necessity of, 120–1, 147

departing guests, imperceptible assistance to, 118–20

disfiguring bodily characteristics, how to ignore, 91

dress sense, tactful interventions with others, 132–3

educated mind, importance of having one, 72–3

evolution, failure to keep up with civilization, 108

exercise, socially acceptable forms of, 160–2

filial duty, knowing how to cope, 39–44

front-doorbell-ringing technique, practising, 23–4

gardening, suitable dressing for, 143, 173–4

gloves, occasions on which to wear, 80, 137, 174

hands, importance of ensuring cleanliness of in tradespersons, 17–18, 21–2

hats, 83, 132, 138–9

health, avoidance of glowing, 159–60

higher education, importance of, 72–3

home, definition of a real, 11–12

husbands, uses of, 148, 156, 169–72

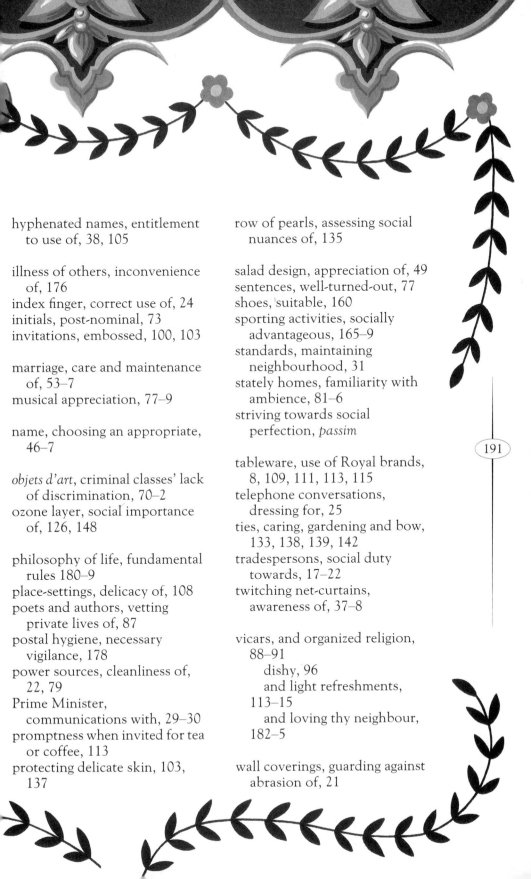

hyphenated names, entitlement to use of, 38, 105

illness of others, inconvenience of, 176
index finger, correct use of, 24
initials, post-nominal, 73
invitations, embossed, 100, 103

marriage, care and maintenance of, 53–7
musical appreciation, 77–9

name, choosing an appropriate, 46–7

objets d'art, criminal classes' lack of discrimination, 70–2
ozone layer, social importance of, 126, 148

philosophy of life, fundamental rules 180–9
place-settings, delicacy of, 108
poets and authors, vetting private lives of, 87
postal hygiene, necessary vigilance, 178
power sources, cleanliness of, 22, 79
Prime Minister, communications with, 29–30
promptness when invited for tea or coffee, 113
protecting delicate skin, 103, 137

row of pearls, assessing social nuances of, 135

salad design, appreciation of, 49
sentences, well-turned-out, 77
shoes, suitable, 160
sporting activities, socially advantageous, 165–9
standards, maintaining neighbourhood, 31
stately homes, familiarity with ambience, 81–6
striving towards social perfection, *passim*

tableware, use of Royal brands, 8, 109, 111, 113, 115
telephone conversations, dressing for, 25
ties, caring, gardening and bow, 133, 138, 139, 142
tradespersons, social duty towards, 17–22
twitching net-curtains, awareness of, 37–8

vicars, and organized religion, 88–91
    dishy, 96
    and light refreshments, 113–15
    and loving thy neighbour, 182–5

wall coverings, guarding against abrasion of, 21

SEMPER IN SPECIEM

ALWAYS FOR THE SAKE OF APPEARANCES